Touching the Risen Christ

Wisdom from The Fathers

Patricia Mitchell, General Editor

D1372001

the WORD®
among us

The Word Among Us Press
9639 Doctor Perry Road
Ijamsville, Maryland   21754
ISBN 0-932085-22-9
www.wau.org

Wisdom Series Editor: Patricia Mitchell
Copy Assistant: Angela Burrin
Design: David Crosson

Table of Contents

Introduction

Introduction

It is all too easy to picture the Church Fathers as an unapproachable group of old men whose voluminous writings have little to say to modern-day Christians. Yet if we could meet one of these men in person, we might find our preconceptions shattered. While their culture and outlook would differ dramatically from our own, we would also discover that we have much in common with them. As fellow Christians, we would be inspired by their passionate love for Christ and their thorough understanding of the truths of the gospel. Many of them would be able to tell us hair-raising adventures of secret flights from persecution and long exiles engineered by heretical bishops.

Just who are the "Fathers"? The church considers them holy men and leaders of early Christianity—from the first through the seventh or eighth century—who left behind important teachings about the faith. In the West, even some early Middle Age saints are considered "Fathers." Many lived in busy cosmopolitan cities like Rome and Alexandria, but others came from Persia, Syria, Gaul and England. They spoke numerous languages, but they were all champions of orthodox Christianity. In their lifetimes, they developed and clarified key points about the Trinity, the Incarnation, salvation, and redemption.

Thoroughly immersed in scripture and prayer, these men used their brilliant minds and their zealous hearts to teach, convert, and explicate. They wrote and preached so that everyone could come to a saving knowledge of Jesus Christ. For example, St. Augustine was converted after hearing the preaching of the Bishop of Milan, St. Ambrose. In the process of defending Christianity against the waves of heresies that rose up over these early centuries, the Church Fathers were able to illuminate basic gospel truths that we can easily take for granted. It was these truths that saw them through a host of trials and struggles, and it is these same truths that can carry us through any difficulty we face in our own lives.

Readers just getting acquainted with the writings of the Church Fathers will notice immediately how they are steeped in scripture. For these men, the Bible was their life blood and compass. Much of their writing consisted of commentaries on biblical books and passages. They often took several verses and interpreted them allegorically or sought to find, beneath the actual letter of the passage, a deeper spiritual meaning. Their use of scripture in this way yielded both interesting insights and profound doctrines. While this style requires some adjustment for today's readers, it also expands a modern-day view of scripture that can tend to be too analytical or historical.

How can reading the Church Fathers help us to grow in our love for the Lord? So much of what the Fathers wrote centered on our salvation through Jesus Christ, which was bought with the price of his blood. These thoughts, as expressed by the saints of the early church, can fill us with gratitude as we realize more fully what God has done for us. As we focus on the basic truths of the Christian faith, we can move from assenting to them on an intellectual level to internalizing them so deeply that they transform our lives.

The Church Fathers were heroic men who willingly laid down their lives to spread the good news. They themselves had been transformed by the knowledge of God's love and mercy, and many who heard their preaching were converted as well. It is our hope at *The Word Among Us Press* that the passion and zeal of the writers in this book will bring readers to a deeper understanding of the Christian faith and to an all-consuming love for the Trinitarian God. May the same words that nourished the early believers bring you the joy of knowing Jesus Christ, who is "the same yesterday and today and forever" (Hebrews 13:8).

Patricia Mitchell
General Editor

1

Born of Water and the Spirit

BAPTISMAL REGENERATION

Saint Justin Martyr

[*From the First Apology in Defense of the Christians*]

Through Christ we received new life and we conse-crated ourselves to God. I will explain the way in which we did this. Those who believe what we teach is true and who give assurance of their ability to live according to that teaching are taught to ask God's forgiveness for their sins by prayer and fasting and we pray and fast with them. We then lead them to a place where there is water and they are reborn in the same way as we were reborn; that is to say, they are washed in the water in the name of God, the Father and Lord of the whole universe, of our Savior Jesus Christ and of the Holy Spirit. This is done because Christ said: *Unless you are born again you will not enter the kingdom of heaven,* and it is obviously impossible for any-one, having once been born, to reenter his mother's womb.

An explanation of how repentant sinners are to be freed from their sins is given through the prophet Isaiah in the words: *Wash yourselves and be clean. Remove the evil from your souls; learn to do what is right. Be just to the orphan, vindicate the widow. Come, let us reason together, says the Lord. If your sins are like scarlet, I will make them white as wool; if they are like crimson, I will make them white as snow. But if you do not heed me, you shall be devoured by the sword. The mouth of the Lord has spoken.*

The apostle taught us the reason for this ceremony of ours. Our first birth took place without our knowledge or consent because our parents came together, and we grew up in the midst of wickedness. So if we were not to remain children of necessity and ignorance, we needed a new birth of which we ourselves would be conscious, and which would be the result of our own free choice. We needed, too, to have our sins forgiven. This is why the name of God, the Father and Lord of the whole universe, is pronounced in the water over anyone who chooses to be born again and who has repented of his sins. The person who leads the candidate for baptism to the font calls upon God by this name alone, for God so far surpasses our powers of description that no one can really give a name to him. Anyone who dares to say that he can must be hopelessly insane.

This baptism is called "illumination" because of the mental enlightenment that is experienced by those who learn these things. The person receiving this enlightenment is also baptized in the name of Jesus Christ, who was crucified under Pontius Pilate, and in the name of the Holy Spirit, who through the prophets foretold everything concerning Jesus. ❧

A New Creation in Christ

Saint Augustine, Bishop
[*From a Sermon*]

I speak to you who have just been reborn in baptism, my little children in Christ, you who are the new offspring of the Church, gift of the Father, proof of Mother Church's fruitfulness. All of you who stand fast in the Lord are a holy seed, a new colony of bees, the very flower of our ministry and fruit of our toil, my joy and my crown. It is the words of the Apostle that I address to you: *Put on the Lord Jesus Christ, and make no provision for the flesh and its desires*, so that you may be clothed with the life of him whom you have put on in this sacrament. *You have all been clothed with Christ by your baptism in him. There is neither Jew nor Greek; there is neither slave nor freeman; there is neither male nor female; you are all one in Christ Jesus.*

Such is the power of this sacrament: it is a sacrament of new life which begins here and now with the forgiveness of all past sins, and will be brought to completion in the resurrection of the dead. *You have been buried with Christ by baptism into death in order that, as Christ has risen from the dead, you also may walk in newness of life.*

You are walking now by faith, still on pilgrimage in a mortal body away from the Lord; but he to whom your steps are directed is himself the sure and certain way for you: Jesus Christ, who for our sake became man. For all who fear him he has stored up abundant happiness, which he will reveal to those who hope in him, bringing it to completion when we have attained the reality which even now we possess in hope.

This is the octave day of your new birth. Today is fulfilled in you the sign of faith that was prefigured in the Old Testament by the circumcision of the flesh on the eighth day after birth. When the Lord rose from the dead, he put off the mortality of the flesh; his risen body was still the same body, but it was no longer subject to death. By his resurrection he consecrated Sunday, or the Lord's day. Though the third after his passion, this day is the eighth after the Sabbath, and thus also the first day of the week.

And so your own hope of resurrection, though not yet realized, is sure and certain, because you have received the Sacrament or sign of this reality, and have been given the pledge of the Spirit. *If, then, you have risen with Christ, seek the things that are above, where Christ is seated at the right hand of God. Set your hearts on heavenly things, not the things that are on earth. For you have died and your life is hidden with Christ in God. When Christ, your life, appears, then you too will appear with him in glory.* ❧

BAPTISM IS A SYMBOL OF CHRIST'S PASSION

Saint Augustine, Bishop
[*From the Jerusalem Catecheses*]

You were led down to the font of holy baptism just as Christ was taken down from the cross and placed in the tomb which is before your eyes. Each of you was asked, "Do you believe in the name of the Father, and of the Son, and of the Holy Spirit?" You made the profession of faith that brings salvation, you were plunged into the water, and three times you rose again. This symbolized the three days Christ spent in the tomb.

As our Savior spent three days and three nights in the depths of the earth, so your first rising from the water represented the first day and your first immersion represented the first night. At night a man cannot see, but in the day he walks in the light. So when you were immersed in the water it was like night for you and you could not see, but when you rose again it was like coming into broad daylight. In the same instant you died and were born again; the saving water was both your tomb and your mother.

Solomon's phrase in another context is very apposite here. He spoke of *a time to give birth, and a time to die.* For you, however, it was the reverse: a time to die, and a time to be born, although in fact both events took place at the same time and your birth was simultaneous with your death.

This is something amazing and unheard of! It was not we who actually died, were buried and rose again. We only did these things symbolically, but we have been saved in actual fact. It is Christ who was crucified, who was buried and who rose again, and all this was been attributed to us. We share in his sufferings symbolically and gain salvation in reality. What boundless love for men! Christ's undefiled hands were pierced by the nails; he suffered the pain. I experience no pain, no anguish, yet by the share that I have in his sufferings he freely grants me salvation.

Let no one imagine that baptism consists only in the forgiveness of sins and in the grace of adoption. Our baptism is not like the baptism of John, which conferred only the forgiveness of sins. We know perfectly well that baptism, besides washing away our sins and bringing us the gift of the Holy Spirit, is a symbol of the sufferings of Christ. This is why Paul exclaims: *Do you not know that when we were baptized into Christ Jesus we were, by that very action, sharing in his death? By baptism we went with him into the tomb.*

By One Death and Resurrection the World Was Saved

Saint Basil
[From the Book "On the Holy Spirit"]

When mankind was estranged from him by disobedience, God our Savior made a plan for raising us from our fall and restoring us to friendship with himself. According to this plan Christ came in the flesh, he showed us the gospel way of life, he suffered, died on the cross, was buried and rose from the dead. He did this so that we could be saved by imitation of him, and recover our original status as sons of God by adoption.

To attain holiness, then, we must not only pattern our lives on Christ's by being gentle, humble and patient, we must also imitate him in his death. Taking Christ for his model, Paul said that he wanted to become like him in his death in the hope that he too would be raised from death to life.

We imitate Christ's death by being buried with him in baptism. If we ask what this kind of burial means and what benefit we may hope to derive from it, it means first of all making a complete break with our former way of life, and our Lord himself said that this cannot be done unless a man is born again. In other words, we have to begin a new life, and we cannot do so until our previous life has been brought to an end. When runners reach the turning point on a racecourse, they have to pause briefly before they can go back in the opposite direction. So also when we wish to reverse the direction of our lives there must be a pause, or a death, to mark the end of one life and the beginning of another.

Our descent into hell takes place when we imitate the burial of Christ by our baptism. The bodies of the baptized are in a sense buried in the water as a symbol of their renunciation of the sins of their unregenerate nature. As the Apostle says: *The circumcision you have undergone is not an operation performed by human hands, but the complete stripping away of your unregenerate nature. This is the circumcision that Christ gave us, and it is accomplished by our burial with him in baptism.* Baptism cleanses the soul from the pollution of worldly thoughts and inclinations. *You will wash me*, says the psalmist, *and I shall be whiter than snow*. We receive this saving baptism only once because there was only one death and one resurrection for the salvation of the world, and baptism is its symbol.

2

Repentance and Mercy

BLESSED ARE THE CLEAN OF HEART,
FOR THEY WILL SEE GOD

Saint Theophilus of Antioch, Bishop
[*From The Book Addressed to Autolycus*]

If you say, "Show me your God," I will say to you, "Show me what kind of person you are, and I will show you my God." Show me then whether the eyes of your mind can see, and the ears of your heart hear.

It is like this. Those who can see with the eyes of their bodies are aware of what is happening in this life on earth. They get to know things that are different from each other. They distinguish light and darkness, black and white, ugliness and beauty, elegance and inelegance, proportion and lack of proportion, excess and defect. The same is true of the sounds we hear: high or low or pleasant. So it is with the ears of our heart and the eyes of our mind in their capacity to hear or see God.

God is seen by those who have the capacity to see him, provided that they keep the eyes of their mind open. All have eyes, but some have eyes that are shrouded in darkness, unable to see the light of the sun.

Because the blind cannot see it, it does not follow that the sun does not shine. The blind must trace the cause back to themselves and their eyes. In the same way, you have eyes in your mind that are shrouded in darkness because of your sins and evil deeds.

A person's soul should be clean, like a mirror reflecting light. If there is rust on the mirror his face cannot be seen in it. In the same way, no one who has sin within him can see God.

But if you will you can be healed. Hand yourself over to the doctor, and he will open the eyes of your mind and heart. Who is to be the doctor? It is God, who heals and gives life through his Word and wisdom. Through his Word and wisdom he created the universe, *for by his Word the heavens were established, and by his Spirit all their array.* His wisdom is supreme. God *by wisdom founded the earth, by understanding he arranged the heavens, by his knowledge the depths broke forth and the clouds poured out the dew.*

If you understand this, and live in purity and holiness and justice, you may see God. But, before all, faith and the fear of God must take the first place in your heart, and then you will understand all this. When you have laid aside mortality and been clothed in immortality, then you will see God according to your merits. God raises up your flesh to immortality along with your soul, and then, once made immortal, you will see the immortal One, if you believe in him now. ❧

REPENT

Saint Clement, Pope
[*From a Letter to the Corinthians*]

Let us fix our attention on the blood of Christ and recognize how precious it is to God his Father, since it was shed for our salvation and brought the grace of repentance to all the world.

If we review the various ages of history, we will see that in every generation the Lord has *offered the opportunity of repentance* to any who were willing to turn to him. When Noah preached God's message of repentance, all who listened to him were saved. Jonah told the Ninevites they were going to be destroyed, but when they repented, their prayers gained God's forgiveness for their sins, and they were saved, even though they were not of God's people.

Under the inspiration of the Holy Spirit, the ministers of God's grace have spoken of repentance; indeed, the Master of the whole universe himself spoke of repentance with an oath: *As I live*, says the Lord, *I do not wish the death of the sinner but his repentance.* He added this evidence of his goodness: *House of Israel, repent of your wickedness. Tell the sons of my people: If their sins should reach from earth to heaven, if they are brighter than scarlet and blacker than sackcloth, you need only turn to me with your whole heart and say, "Father," and I will listen to you as to a holy people.*

In other words, God wanted all his beloved ones to have the opportunity to repent and he confirmed this desire by his own almighty will. That is why we should obey his sovereign and glorious will and prayerfully entreat his mercy and kindness. We should be suppliant before him and turn to his compassion, rejecting empty works and quarreling and jealousy which only lead to death.

Brothers, we should be humble in mind, putting aside all arrogance, pride and foolish anger. Rather, we should act in accordance with the Scriptures, as the Holy Spirit says: *The wise man must not glory in his wisdom nor the strong man in his strength nor the rich man in his riches. Rather, let him who glories glory in the Lord by seeking him and doing what is right and just.* Recall especially what the Lord Jesus said when he taught gentleness and forbearance. *Be merciful,* he said, *so that you may have mercy shown to you. Forgive, so that you may be forgiven. As you treat others, so you will be treated. As you give, so you will receive. As you judge, so you will be judged. As you are kind to others, so you will be treated kindly. The measure of your giving will be the measure of your receiving.*

Let these commandments and precepts strengthen us to live in humble obedience to his sacred words. As Scripture asks: *Whom shall I look upon with favor except the humble, peaceful man who trembles at my words?*

Sharing then in the heritage of so many vast and glorious achievements, let us hasten toward the goal of peace, set before us from the beginning. Let us keep our eyes firmly fixed on the Father and Creator of the whole universe, and hold fast to his splendid and transcendent gifts of peace and all his blessings. ❧

The Mercy of God to the Penitent

Saint Maximus the Confessor, Abbot
[*From a Letter*]

God's will is to save us, and nothing pleases him more than our coming back to him with true repentance. The heralds of truth and the ministers of divine grace have told us this from the beginning, repeating it in every age. Indeed, God's desire for our salvation is the primary and preeminent sign of his infinite goodness. It was precisely in order to show that there is nothing closer to God's heart that the divine Word of God the Father, with untold condescension, lived among us in the flesh, and did, suffered, and said all that was necessary to reconcile us to God the Father, when we were at enmity with him, and to restore us to the life of blessedness from which we had been exiled. He healed our physical infirmities by miracles; he freed us from our sins, many and grievous as they were, by suffering and dying, taking them upon himself as if he were answerable for them, sinless though he was. He also taught us in many different ways that we should wish to imitate him by our own kindness and genuine love for one another.

So it was that Christ proclaimed that he had come to call sinners to repentance, not the righteous, and that it was not the healthy who required a doctor, but the sick. He declared that he had come to look for the sheep that was lost, and that it was to the lost sheep of the house of Israel that he had been sent. Speaking more obscurely in the parable of the silver coin, he tells us that the purpose of his coming was to reclaim the royal image, which had become coated with the filth of sin. *You can be sure that there is joy in heaven*, he said, *over one sinner who repents*.

To give the same lesson he revived the man who, having fallen into the hands of brigands, had been left stripped and half-dead from his wounds; he poured wine and oil on the wounds, bandaged them, placed the man on his own mule and brought him to an inn, where he left sufficient money to have him cared for, and promised to repay any further expense on his return.

Again, he told of how that Father, who is goodness itself, was moved with pity for his profligate son who returned and made amends by repentance; how he embraced him, dressed him once more in the fine garments that befitted his own dignity, and did not reproach him for any of his sins.

So too, when he found wandering in the mountains and hills the one sheep that had strayed from God's flock of a hundred, he brought it back to the fold, but he did not exhaust it by driving it ahead of him. Instead, he placed it on his own shoulders and so, compassionately, he restored it safely to the flock.

So also he cried out: *Come to me, all you that toil and are heavy of heart. Accept my yoke,* he said, by which he meant his commands, or rather, the whole way of life that he taught us in the Gospel. He then speaks of a burden, but that is only because repentance seems difficult. In fact, however, *my yoke is easy,* he assures us, *and my burden is light.*

Then again he instructs us in divine justice and goodness, telling us to be like our heavenly Father, holy, perfect and merciful. *Forgive,* he says, *and you will be forgiven. Behave toward other people as you would wish them to behave toward you.* ◈

GOD'S MERCY HAS BEEN EXTENDED TO ALL; THE WHOLE WORLD HAS BEEN SAVED

Saint Cyril of Alexandria, Bishop
[*From the Commentary on the Letter to the Romans*]

Though many, we are one body, and members one of another, united by Christ in the bonds of love. *Christ has made Jews and Gentiles one by breaking down the barrier that divided us and abolishing the law with its precepts and decrees.* This is why we should all be of one mind and if one members suffers some misfortune, all should suffer with him; if one member is honored, all should be glad.

Paul says: Accept one another as Christ accepted you, for the glory of God. Now accepting one another means being willing to share one another's thoughts and feelings, bearing one another's burdens, and *preserving the unity of the Spirit in the bond of peace.* This is how God accepted us in Christ, for John's testimony is true and he said that *God* the Father *loved the world so much that he gave his own Son for us.* God's Son was given as a ransom for the lives of us all. He has delivered us from death, redeemed us from death and from sin.

Paul throws light on the purpose of God's plan when he says that Christ became the servant of the circumcised to show God's fidelity. God had promised the Jewish patriarchs that he would bless their offspring and make it as numerous as the stars of heaven. This is why the divine Word himself, who as God holds all creation in being and is the source of its well-being, appeared in the flesh and became man. He came into this world in human flesh not to be served, but, as he himself said, to serve and to give his life as a ransom for many.

Christ declared that his coming in visible form was to fulfill the promise made to Israel. *I was sent only to the lost sheep of the house of Israel,* he said. Paul was perfectly correct, then, in saying that Christ became a servant of the circumcised in order to fulfill the promise made to the patriarchs and that God the Father had charged him with this task, as also with the task of bringing salvation to the Gentiles, so that they too might praise their Savior and Redeemer as the Creator of the universe. In this way God's mercy has been extended to all men, including the Gentiles, and it can be seen that the mystery of the divine wisdom contained in Christ has not failed in its benevolent purpose. In the place of those who fell away the whole world has been saved. ◈

3

Prayer, Fasting, and Almsgiving

PRAYER KNOCKS, FASTING OBTAINS, MERCY RECEIVES

Saint Peter Chrysologus, Bishop
[*From a Sermon*]

There are three things, my brethren, by which faith stands firm, devotion remains constant, and virtue endures. They are prayer, fasting and mercy. Prayer knocks at the door, fasting obtains, mercy receives. Prayer, mercy and fasting: these three are one, and they give life to each other.

Fasting is the soul of prayer, mercy is the lifeblood of fasting. Let no one try to separate them, they cannot be separated. If you have only one of them or not all together, you have nothing. So if you pray, fast; if you fast, show mercy; if you want your petition to be heard, hear the petition of others. If you do not close your ear to others you open God's ear to yourself.

When you fast, see the fasting of others. If you want God to know that you are hungry, know that another is hungry. If you hope for mercy, show mercy. If you look for kindness, show kindness. If you want to receive, give.

If you ask for yourself what you deny to others, your asking is a mockery.

Let this be the pattern for all men when they practice mercy: show mercy to others in the same way, with the same generosity, with the same promptness, as you want others to show mercy to you.

Therefore, let prayer, mercy and fasting be one single plea to God on our behalf, one speech in our defense, a threefold united prayer in our favor.

Let us use fasting to make up for what we have lost by despising others. Let us offer our souls in sacrifice by means of fasting. There is nothing more pleasing that we can offer to God, as the psalmist said in prophecy: *A sacrifice to God is a broken spirit; God does not despise a bruised and humbled heart.*

Offer your soul to God, make him an oblation of your fasting, so that your soul may be a pure offering, a holy sacrifice, a living victim, remaining your own and at the same time made over to God. Whoever fails to give this to God will not be excused, for if you are to give him yourself you are never without the means of giving.

To make these acceptable, mercy must be added. Fasting bears no fruit unless it is watered by mercy. Fasting dries up when mercy dries up. Mercy is to fasting as rain is to the earth. However much you may cultivate your heart, clear the soil of your nature, root out vices, sow virtues, if you do not release the springs of mercy, your fasting will bear no fruit.

When you fast, if your mercy is thin your harvest will be thin; when you fast, what you pour out in mercy overflows into your barn. Therefore, do not lose by saving, but gather in by scattering. Give to the poor, and you give to yourself. You will not be allowed to keep what you have refused to give to others. ❧

PURIFICATION OF SPIRIT THROUGH FASTING AND ALMSGIVING

Saint Leo the Great, Pope
[*From a Sermon*]

Dear friends, at every moment *the earth is full of the mercy of God*, and nature itself is a lesson for all the faithful in the worship of God. The heavens, the sea and all that is in them bear witness to the goodness and omnipotence of their Creator, and the marvelous beauty of the elements as they obey him demands from the intelligent creation a fitting expression of its gratitude.

But with the return of that season marked out in a special way by the mystery of our redemption, and of the days that lead up to the paschal feast, we are summoned more urgently to prepare ourselves by a purification of spirit.

The special note of the paschal feast is this: the whole Church rejoices in the forgiveness of sins. It rejoices in the forgiveness not only of those who are then reborn in holy baptism but also of those who are already numbered among God's adopted children.

Initially, men are made new by the rebirth of baptism.

Yet there is still required a daily renewal to repair the shortcomings of our mortal nature, and whatever degree of progress has been made there is no one who should not be more advanced. All must therefore strive to ensure that on the day of redemption no one may be found in the sins of his former life.

Dear friends, what the Christian should be doing at all times should be done now with greater care and devotion, so that the Lenten fast enjoined by the apostles may be fulfilled, not simply by abstinence from food but above all by the renunciation of sin.

There is no more profitable practice as a companion to holy and spiritual fasting than that of almsgiving. This embraces under the single name of mercy many excellent works of devotion, so that the good intentions of all the faithful may be of equal value, even where their means are not. The love that we owe both God and man is always free from any obstacle that would prevent us from having a good intention. The angels sang: *Glory to God in the highest, and peace to his people on earth.* The person who shows love and compassion to those in any kind of affliction is blessed, not only with the virtue of good will but also with the gift of peace.

The works of mercy are innumerable. Their very variety brings this advantage to those who are true Christians, that in the matter of almsgiving not only the rich and affluent but also those of average means and the poor are able to play their part. Those who are unequal in their capacity to give can be equal in the love within their hearts. ❧

JESUS CHRIST PRAYS FOR US AND IN US
AND IS THE OBJECT OF OUR PRAYERS

Saint Augustine, Bishop
[*From a Commentary on the Psalms*]

God could give no greater gift to men than to make his Word, through whom he created all things, their head and to join them to him as his members, so that the Word might be both Son of God and son of man, one God with the Father, and one man with all men. The result is that when we speak with God in prayer we do not separate the Son from him, and when the body of the Son prays it does not separate its head from itself: it is the one Savior of his body, our Lord Jesus Christ, the Son of God, who prays for us and in us and is himself the object of our prayers.

He prays for us as our priest, he prays in us as our head, he is the object of our prayers as our God.

Let us then recognize both our voice in his, and his voice in ours. When something is said, especially in prophecy, about the Lord Jesus Christ that seems to belong to a condition of lowliness unworthy of God, we must not hesitate to ascribe this condition to one who did not hesitate to unite himself with us. Every creature is his servant, for it was through him that every creature came to be.

We contemplate his glory and divinity when we listen to these words: *In the beginning was the Word, and the*

Word was with God, and the Word was God. He was in the beginning with God. All things were made through him, and without him nothing was made. Here we gaze on the divinity of the Son of God, something supremely great and surpassing all the greatness of his creatures. Yet in other parts of Scripture we hear him as one sighing, praying, giving praise and thanks.

We hesitate to attribute these words to him because our minds are slow to come down to his humble level when we have just been contemplating him in his divinity. It is as though we were doing him an injustice in acknowledging in a man the words of one with whom we spoke when we prayed to God; we are usually at a loss and try to change the meaning. Yet our minds find nothing in Scripture that does not go back to him, nothing that will allow us to stray from him.

Our thoughts must then be awakened to keep their vigil of faith. We must realize that the one whom we were contemplating a short time before in his nature as God took to himself the nature of a servant; he was made in the likeness of men and found to be a man like others; he humbled himself by being obedient even to accepting death; as he hung on the cross he made the psalmist's words his own: *My God, my God, why have you forsaken me?*

We pray to him as God, he prays for us as a servant. In the first case he is the Creator, in the second a creature. Himself unchanged, he took to himself our created nature in order to change it, and made us one man with himself, head and body. We pray then to him, through him, in him, and we speak along with him and he along with us. ∽

THE SPIRITUAL OFFERING OF PRAYER

Tertullian, Priest
[*From the Treatise "On Prayer"*]

Prayer is the offering in spirit that has done away with the sacrifices of old. *What good do I receive from the multiplicity of your sacrifices?* asks God. *I have had enough of burnt offerings of rams, and I do not want the fat of lambs and the blood of bulls and goats. Who has asked for these from your hands?*

What God has asked for we learn from the Gospel. *The hour will come*, he says, *when true worshipers will worship the Father in spirit and in truth. God is a spirit*, and so he looks for worshipers who are like himself.

We are true worshipers and true priests. We pray in spirit, and so offer in spirit the sacrifice of prayer. Prayer is an offering that belongs to God and is acceptable to him: it is the offering he has asked for, the offering he planned as his own.

We must dedicate this offering with our whole heart, we must fatten it on faith, tend it by truth, keep it unblemished through innocence and clean through chastity, and crown it with love. We must escort it to the altar of God in a procession of good works to the sound of psalms and hymns. Then it will gain for us all that we ask of God.

Since God asks for prayer offered in spirit and in truth, how can he deny anything to this kind of prayer? How great is the evidence of its power, as we read and hear and believe.

Of old, prayer was able to rescue from fire and beasts and hunger, even before it received its perfection from Christ. How much greater then is the power of Christian prayer. No longer does prayer bring an angel of comfort to the heart of a fiery furnace, or close up the mouths of lions, or transport to the hungry food from the fields. No longer does it remove all sense of pain by the grace it wins for others. But it gives the armor of patience to those who suffer, who feel pain, who are distressed. It strengthens the power of grace, so that faith may know what it is gaining from the Lord, and understand what it is suffering for the name of God.

In the past prayer was able to bring down punishment, rout armies, withhold the blessing of rain. Now, however, the prayer of the just turns aside the whole anger of God, keeps vigil for its enemies, pleads for persecutors. Is it any wonder that it can call down water from heaven when it could obtain fire from heaven as well? Prayer is the one thing that can conquer God. But Christ has willed that it should work no evil, and has given it all power over good.

Its only art is to call back the souls of the dead from the very journey into death, to give strength to the weak, to heal the sick, to exorcise the possessed, to open prison cells, to free the innocent from their chains. Prayer cleanses from sin, drives away temptations, stamps out persecutions, comforts the fainthearted, gives new strength to the courageous, brings travelers safely home, calms the waves, confounds robbers, feeds the poor, over-rules the rich, lifts up the fallen, supports those who are falling, sustains those who stand firm.

All the angels pray. Every creature prays. Cattle and wild beasts pray and bend the knee. As they come from their barns and caves they look up to heaven and call out, lifting up their spirit in their own fashion. The birds too rise and lift themselves up to heaven: they open out their wings, instead of hands, in the form of a cross, and give voice to what seems to be a prayer.

What more need be said on the duty of prayer? Even the Lord himself prayed. To him be honor and power for ever and ever. Amen. ∾

PRAYER IS THE LIGHT OF THE SPIRIT

Saint John Chrysostom, Bishop
[*From a Homily*]

Prayer and converse with God is a supreme good: it is a partnership and union with God. As the eyes of the body are enlightened when they see light, so our spirit, when it is intent on God, is illumined by his infinite light. I do not mean the prayer of outward observance but prayer from the heart, not confined to fixed times or periods but continuous throughout the day and night.

Our spirit should be quick to reach out toward God, not only when it is engaged in meditation; at other times also, when it is carrying out its duties, caring for the needy, performing works of charity, giving generously in the service of others, our spirit should long for God and call him to mind, so that these works may be seasoned with the salt of God's love, and so make a palatable offering to the Lord of the universe. Throughout the whole of our lives we may enjoy the benefit that comes from prayer if we devote a great deal of time to it.

Prayer is the light of the spirit, true knowledge of God, mediating between God and man. The spirit, raised up to heaven by prayer, clings to God with the utmost tenderness; like a child crying tearfully for its mother, it craves the milk that God provides. It seeks the satisfaction of its own desires, and receives gifts outweighing the whole world of nature.

Prayer stands before God as an honored ambassador. It gives joy to the spirit, peace to the heart. I speak of prayer, not words. It is the longing for God, love too deep for words, a gift not given by man but by God's grace. The apostle Paul says: *We do not know how we are to pray but the Spirit himself pleads for us with inexpressible longings*.

When the Lord gives this kind of prayer to a man, he gives him riches that cannot be taken away, heavenly food that satisfies the spirit. One who tastes this food is set on fire with an eternal longing for the Lord: his spirit burns as in a fire of the utmost intensity.

Practice prayer from the beginning. Paint your house with the colors of modesty and humility. Make it radiant with the light of justice. Decorate it with the finest gold leaf of good deeds. Adorn it with the walls and stones of faith and generosity. Crown it with the pinnacle of prayer. In this way you will make it a perfect dwelling place for the Lord. You will be able to receive him as in a splendid palace, and through his grace you will already possess him, his image enthroned in the temple of your spirit. ❧

4

The Sacrificial Lamb

CHRIST GAVE HIS OWN BODY FOR THE LIFE OF ALL MEN

Saint Cyril of Alexandria, Bishop
[*From a Commentary on the Gospel of John*]

I am dying for all men," says the Lord. "I am dying to give them life through myself and to redeem the whole human race through my humanity. In my death, death itself will die and man's fallen nature will rise again with me. I wanted to be like my brothers in every respect, so I became a man like you, a descendant of Abraham." Understanding this well Saint Paul says: *As the children of a family share the same flesh and blood, he too shared our human nature so that by his death he could destroy the power of the devil, the prince of death.* Death itself and the prince of death could be destroyed only by Christ, who is above all, giving himself up as a ransom for all.

And so, speaking as a spotless victim offering himself for us to God the Father, Christ says in one of the psalms: *You desired no sacrifices or offerings, but you have prepared a body for me. You took no pleasure in holocausts or sin offerings. Then I said, "Behold, I am coming."* He was crucified for all, desiring his one death for all to give all of us life in him. It was impossible for him to be conquered by death; nor could he who by his very nature is life be subject to corruption. Yet we know that Christ offered his flesh for the life of the world from his own prayer, *Holy Father, protect them*, and from his words, *For their sake I consecrate myself*. By saying that he consecrates himself he means that he offers himself to God as a spotless and sweet-smelling sacrifice. According to the law, anything offered upon the altar was consecrated and considered holy. So Christ gave his own body for the life of all, and makes it the channel through which life flows once more into us. How he does this I will explain to the best of my ability.

When the life-giving Word of God dwelt in human flesh, he changed it into that good thing which is distinctively his, namely, life; and by being wholly united to the flesh in a way beyond our comprehension, he gave it the life-giving power which he has by his very nature. Therefore, the body of Christ gives life to those who receive it. Its presence in mortal men expels death and drives away corruption because it contains within itself in his entirety the Word who totally abolishes corruption. ॐ

THE POWER OF CHRIST'S BLOOD

Saint John Chrysostom, Bishop
[*From the Catecheses*]

If we wish to understand the power of Christ's blood, we should go back to the ancient account of its prefiguration in Egypt. *Sacrifice a lamb without blemish*, commanded Moses, *and sprinkle its blood on your doors*. If we were to ask him what he meant, and how the blood of an irrational beast could possibly save men endowed with reason, his answer would be that the saving power lies not in the blood itself, but in the fact that it is a sign of the Lord's blood. In those days, when the destroying angel saw the blood on the doors he did not dare to enter, so how much less will the devil approach now when he sees, not that figurative blood on the doors, but the true blood on the lips of believers, the doors of the temple of Christ.

If you desire further proof of the power of this blood, remember where it came from, how it came down from the cross, flowing from the Master's side. The gospel records that when Christ was dead, but still hung on the cross, a soldier came and pierced his side with a lance and immediately there poured out water and blood. Now the water was a symbol of baptism and the blood, of the holy eucharist. The soldier pierced the Lord's side, he breached the wall of the sacred temple, and I have found the treasure and made it my own. So also with the lamb: the Jews sacrificed the victim and I have been saved by it.

There flowed from his side water and blood. Beloved, do not pass over this mystery without thought; it has yet another hidden meaning, which I will explain to you. I said that water and blood symbolized baptism and the holy eucharist. From these two sacraments the Church is born: from baptism, *the cleansing water that gives rebirth and renewal through the Holy Spirit,* and from the holy eucharist. Since the symbols of baptism and the eucharist flowed from his side, it was from his side that Christ fashioned the Church, as he had fashioned Eve from the side of Adam. Moses gives a hint of this when he tells the story of the first man and makes him exclaim: *Bone from my bones and flesh from my flesh!* As God then took a rib from Adam's side to fashion a woman, so Christ has given us blood and water from his side to fashion the Church. God took the rib when Adam was in a deep sleep, and in the same way Christ gave us the blood and the water after his own death.

Do you understand, then, how Christ has united his bride to himself and what food he gives us all to eat? By one and the same food we are both brought into being and nourished. As a woman nourishes her child with her own blood and milk, so does Christ unceasingly nourish with his own blood those to whom he himself has given life. ❧

The Lord Descends into Hell

From an Ancient Homily on Holy Saturday

Something strange is happening — there is a great silence on earth today, a great silence and stillness. The whole earth keeps silence because the King is asleep. The earth trembled and is still because God has fallen asleep in the flesh and he has raised up all who have slept ever since the world began. God has died in the flesh and hell trembles with fear.

He has gone to search for our first parent, as for a lost sheep. Greatly desiring to visit those who live in darkness and in the shadow of death, he has gone to free from sorrow the captives Adam and Eve, he who is both God and son of Eve. The Lord approached them bearing the cross, the weapon that had won him the victory. At the sight of him Adam, the first man he had created, struck his breast in terror and cried out to everyone: "My Lord be with you all." Christ answered him: "And with your spirit." He took him by the hand and raised him up saying: "Awake, O sleeper, and rise from the dead, and Christ will give you light."

I am your God, who for your sake have become your son. Out of love for you and for your descendants I now by my own authority command all who are held in bondage to come forth, all who are in darkness to be enlightened, all who are sleeping to arise. I order you, O sleeper, to awake. I did not create you to be held a prisoner in hell. Rise from the dead, for I am the life of the dead. Rise up, work of my hands, you who were created in my image. Rise, let us leave this place, for you are in me and I am in you; together we form only one person and we cannot be separated.

For your sake I, your God, became your son; I, the Lord, took the form of a slave; I, whose home is above the heavens, descended to the earth and beneath the earth. For your sake, for the sake of man, I became like a man without help, free among the dead. For the sake of you, who left a garden, I was betrayed to the Jews in a garden, and I was crucified in a garden.

See on my face the spittle I received in order to restore to you the life I once breathed into you. See there the marks of the blows I received in order to refashion your warped nature in my image. On my back see the marks of the scourging I endured to remove the burden of sin that weighs upon your back. See my hands, nailed firmly to a tree, for you who once wickedly stretched out your hand to a tree.

I slept on the cross and a sword pierced my side for you who slept in paradise and brought forth Eve from your side. My side has healed the pain in yours. My sleep will rouse you from your sleep in hell. The sword that pierced me has sheathed the sword that was turned against you.

Rise, let us leave this place. The enemy led you out of the earthly paradise. I will not restore you to that paradise, but I will enthrone you in heaven. I forbade you the tree that was only a symbol of life, but see, I who am life itself am now one with you. I appointed cherubim to guard you as slaves are guarded, but now I make them worship you as God. The throne formed by cherubim awaits you, its bearers swift and eager. The bridal chamber is adorned, the banquet is ready, the eternal dwelling places are prepared, the treasure houses of all good things lie open. The kingdom of heaven has been prepared for you from all eternity. ❧

THE LAMB THAT WAS SLAIN HAS DELIVERED US FROM DEATH AND GIVEN US LIFE

Saint Melito of Sardis, Bishop
[*From an Easter Homily*]

There was much proclaimed by the prophets about the mystery of the Passover; that mystery is Christ, and to him be glory for ever and ever. Amen.

For the sake of suffering humanity he came down from heaven to earth, clothed himself in that humanity in the Virgin's womb, and was born a man. Having then a body capable of suffering, he took the pain of fallen man upon himself; he triumphed over the diseases of soul and body that were its cause, and by his Spirit, which was incapable of dying, he dealt man's destroyer, death, a fatal blow.

He was led forth like a lamb; he was slaughtered like a sheep. He ransomed us from our servitude to the world, as he had ransomed Israel from the land of Egypt; he freed us from our slavery to the devil, as he had freed Israel from the hand of Pharaoh. He sealed our souls with his own Spirit, and the members of our body with his own blood.

He is the One who covered death with shame and cast the devil into mourning, as Moses cast Pharaoh into mourning. He is the One who smote sin and robbed iniquity of offspring, as Moses robbed the Egyptians of their offspring. He is the One who brought us out of slavery into freedom, out of darkness into light, out of death into life, out of tyranny into an eternal kingdom; who made us a new priesthood, a people chosen to be his own for ever. He is the Passover that is our salvation.

It is he who endured every kind of suffering in all those who foreshadowed him. In Abel he was slain, in Isaac bound, in Jacob exiled, in Joseph sold, in Moses exposed to die. He was sacrificed in the Passover lamb, persecuted in David, dishonored in the prophets.

It is he who was made man of the Virgin, he who was hung on the tree; it is he who was buried in the earth, raised from the dead, and taken up to the heights of heaven. He is the mute lamb, the slain lamb, the lamb born of Mary, the fair ewe. He was seized from the flock, dragged off to be slaughtered, sacrificed in the evening, and buried at night. On the tree no bone of his was broken; in the earth his body knew no decay. He is the One who rose from the dead, and who raised man from the depths of the tomb. ∿

BLESSED IS HE WHO COMES IN THE NAME OF THE LORD. BLESSED IS THE KING OF ISRAEL.

Saint Andrew of Crete, Bishop
[*From a Sermon*]

Let us go together to meet Christ on the Mount of Olives. Today he returns from Bethany and proceeds of his own free will toward his holy and blessed passion, to consummate the mystery of our salvation. He who came down from heaven to raise us from the depths of sin, to raise us with himself, we are told in Scripture, *above every sovereignty, authority and power, and every other name that can be named,* now comes of his own free will to make his journey to Jerusalem. He comes without pomp or ostentation. As the psalmist says: *He will not dispute or raise his voice to make it heard in the streets.* He will be meek and humble, and he will make his entry in simplicity.

Let us run to accompany him as he hastens toward his passion, and imitate those who met him then, not by covering his path with garments, olive branches or palms, but by doing all we can to prostrate ourselves before him by being humble and by trying to live as he would wish. Then we shall be able to receive the Word at his coming, and God, whom no limits can contain, will be within us.

In his humility Christ entered the dark regions of our fallen world and he is glad that he became so humble for our sake, glad that he came and lived among us and shared in our nature in order to raise us up again to himself. And even though we are told that he has now ascended above the highest heavens — the proof, surely, of his power and godhead — his love for man will never rest until he has raised our earthbound nature from glory to glory, and made it one with his own in heaven.

So let us spread before his feet, not garments or soulless olive branches, which delight the eye for a few hours and then wither, but ourselves, clothed in his grace, or rather, clothed completely in him. We who have been baptized into Christ must ourselves be the garments that we spread before him. Now that the crimson stains of our sins have been washed away in the saving waters of baptism and we have become white as pure wool, let us present the conqueror of death, not with mere branches of palms but with the real rewards of his victory. Let our souls take the place of the welcoming branches as we join today in the children's holy song: *Blessed is he who comes in the name of the Lord. Blessed is the king of Israel.* ❧

CHRIST OFFERED HIMSELF FOR US

Saint Fulgentius of Ruspe, Bishop
[*From a Treatise on Faith Addressed to Peter*]

The sacrifices of animal victims which our forefathers were commanded to offer to God by the holy Trinity itself, the one God of the old and new testaments, foreshadowed the most acceptable gift of all. This was the offering which in his compassion the only Son of God would make of himself in his human nature for our sake.

The Apostle teaches that Christ offered *himself for us to God as a fragrant offering and sacrifice*. He is the true God and the true high priest who for our sake entered once for all into the holy of holies, taking with him not the blood of bulls and goats but his own blood. This was fore-shadowed by the high priest of old when each year he took blood and entered the holy of holies.

Christ is therefore the one who in himself alone embodied all that he knew to be necessary to achieve our redemption. He is at once priest and sacrifice, God and temple. He is the priest through whom we have been rec-onciled, the sacrifice by which we have been reconciled, the temple in which we have been reconciled, the God with whom we have been reconciled. He alone is priest, sacrifice and temple because he is all these things as God in the form of a servant; but he is not alone as God, for he is this with the Father and the Holy Spirit in the form of God.

Hold fast to this and never doubt it: the only-begot-ten Son, God the Word, becoming man offered himself for us to God as a fragrant offering and sacrifice. In the time of the old testament, patriarchs, prophets and priests sacrificed animals in his honor, and in honor of the Father and the Holy Spirit as well. Now in the time of the new testament the holy catholic Church throughout the world never ceases to offer the sacrifice of bread and wine, in faith and love, to him and to the Father and the Holy Spirit, with whom he shares one godhead.

Those animal sacrifices foreshadowed the flesh of Christ which he would offer for our sins, though himself without sin, and the blood which he would pour out for the forgiveness of our sins. In this sacrifice there is thanksgiving for, and commemoration of, the flesh of Christ that he offered for us, and the blood that the same God poured out for us. On this Saint Paul says in the Acts of the Apostles: *Keep watch over yourselves and over the whole flock, in which the Holy Spirit has appointed you as bishops to rule the Church of God, which he won for himself by his blood.*

Those sacrifices of old pointed in sign to what was to be given to us. In this sacrifice we see plainly what has already been given to us. Those sacrifices foretold the death of the son of God for sinners. In this sacrifice he is proclaimed as already slain for sinners, as the Apostle testifies: *Christ died for the wicked at a time when we were still powerless, and when we were enemies we were reconciled with God through the death of his Son.* ❧

CHRIST THE HIGH PRIEST MAKES ATONEMENT FOR OUR SINS

Origen, Priest

[*From a Homily on Leviticus*]

Once a year the high priest, leaving the people outside, entered that place where no one except the high priest might enter. In it was the mercy-seat, and above the mercy-seat the cherubim, as well as the ark of the covenant and the altar of incense.

Let me turn to my true high priest, the Lord Jesus Christ. In our human nature he spent the whole year in the company of the people, the year that he spoke of when he said: *He sent me to bring good news to the poor, to announce the acceptable year of the Lord, and the day of forgiveness.* Notice how once in that year, on the day of atonement, he enters into the holy of holies. Having fulfilled God's plan, he passes through the heavens and enters into the presence of the Father to make him turn in mercy to the human race and to pray for all who believe in him.

John the apostle, knowing of the atonement that Christ makes to the Father for all men, says this: *Little children, I say these things so that you may not sin. But if we have sinned we have an advocate with the Father, Jesus Christ, the just one. He is the atonement for our sins.* In the same way Paul refers to this atonement when he says of Christ: *God appointed him to be the atonement for our sins in his blood, through faith.* We have then a day of atonement that remains until the world comes to an end.

God's word tells us: *The high priest shall put incense on the fire in the sight of the Lord. The smoke of the incense shall cover the mercy-seat above the tokens of the covenant, so that he may not die. He shall take some of the blood of the bull-calf and sprinkle it with his finger over the mercy-seat toward the east.*

God taught the people of the old covenant how to celebrate the ritual offered to him in atonement for the sins of men. But you have come to Christ, the true high priest. Through his blood he has made God turn to you in mercy and has reconciled you with the Father. You must not think simply of ordinary blood but you must learn to recognize instead the blood of the Word. Listen to him as he tells you: *This is my blood, which will be shed for you for the forgiveness of sins.*

There is a deeper meaning in the fact that the high priest sprinkles the blood toward the east. Atonement comes to you from the east. From the east comes the one whose name is Dayspring, he who is mediator between God and men. You are invited then to look always to the east: it is there that the sun of righteousness rises for you, it is there that the light is always being born for you. You are never to walk in darkness; the great and final day is not to enfold you in darkness. Do not let the night and mist of ignorance steal upon you. So that you may always enjoy the light of knowledge, keep always in the daylight of faith, hold fast always to the light of love and peace. ✎

IT WAS NECESSARY THAT CHRIST SHOULD SUFFER AND SO ENTER INTO HIS GLORY

Saint Anastasius of Antioch
[*From a Discourse*]

Christ, who has shown by his words and actions that he was truly God and Lord of the universe, said to his disciples as he was about to go up to Jerusalem: *We are going up to Jerusalem now, and the Son of Man will be handed over to the Gentiles and the chief priests and scribes to be scourged and mocked and crucified.*

These words bore out the predictions of the prophets, who had foretold the death he was to die in Jerusalem. From the beginning holy Scripture had foretold Christ's death, the sufferings that would precede it, and what would happen to his body afterward. Scripture also affirmed that these things were going to happen to one who was immortal and incapable of suffering because he was God.

Only by reflecting upon the meaning of the incarnation can we see how it is possible to say with perfect truth both that Christ suffered and that he was incapable of suffering, and why the Word of God, in himself incapable of suffering, came to suffer. In fact, man could have been saved in no other way, as Christ alone knew and those to whom he revealed it. For he knows all the secrets of the Father, even as *the Spirit penetrates the depths of all mysteries.*

It was necessary for Christ to suffer: his passion was absolutely unavoidable. He said so himself when he called his companions dull and slow to believe because they failed to recognize that he had to suffer and so enter into his glory. Leaving behind him the glory that had been his with the Father before the world was made, he had gone forth to save his people. This salvation, however, could be achieved only by the suffering of the author of our life, as Paul taught when he said that *the author of life himself was made perfect through suffering.* Because of us he was deprived of his glory for a little while, the glory that was his as the Father's only-begotten Son, but through the cross this glory is seen to have been restored to him in a certain way in the body that he had assumed. Explaining what water the Savior referred to when he said: *He that has faith in me shall have rivers of living water flowing from within him,* John says in his gospel that *he was speaking of the Holy Spirit which those who believed in him were to receive, for the Spirit had not yet been given because Jesus had not yet been glorified.* The glorification he meant was his death upon the cross for which the Lord prayed to the Father before undergoing his passion, asking his Father to give him the glory that he had in his presence before the world began. ❧

WE KEEP THE COMING FEAST OF THE LORD THROUGH DEEDS, NOT WORDS

Saint Athanasius, Bishop
[*From an Easter Letter*]

The Word who became all things for us is close to us, our Lord Jesus Christ who promises to remain with us always. He cries out, saying: *See, I am with you all the days of this age.* He is himself the shepherd, the high priest, the way and the door, and has become all things at once for us. In the same way, he has come among us as our feast and holy day as well. The blessed Apostle says of him who was awaited: *Christ has been sacrificed as our Passover*. It was Christ who shed his light on the psalmist as he prayed: *You are my joy, deliver me from those surrounding me*. True joy, genuine festival, means the casting out of wickedness. To achieve this one must live a life of perfect goodness and, in the serenity of the fear of God, practice contemplation in one's heart.

This was the way of the saints, who in their lifetime and at every stage of life rejoiced as at a feast. Blessed David, for example, not once but seven times rose at night to win God's favor through prayer. The great Moses was full of joy as he sang God's praises in hymns of victory for the defeat of Pharaoh and the oppressors of the Hebrew people. Others had hearts filled always with gladness as they performed their sacred duty of worship, like the great Samuel and the blessed Elijah. Because of their holy lives they gained freedom, and now keep festival in heaven. They rejoice after their pilgrimage in shadows, and now distinguish the reality from the promise.

When we celebrate the feast in our own day, what path are we to take? As we draw near to this feast, who is to be our guide? Beloved, it must be none other than the one whom you will address with me as our Lord Jesus Christ. He says: *I am the way*. As blessed John tells us: it is Christ *who takes away the sin of the world*. It is he who purifies our souls, as the prophet Jeremiah says: *Stand upon the ways; look and see which is the good path, and you will find in it the way of amendment for your souls*.

In former times the blood of goats and the ashes of a

calf were sprinkled on those who were unclean, but they were able to purify only the body. Now through the grace of God's Word everyone is made abundantly clean. If we follow Christ closely we shall be allowed, even on this earth, to stand as it were on the threshold of the heavenly Jerusalem, and enjoy the contemplation of that everlasting feast, like the blessed apostles, who in following the Savior as their leader, showed, and still show, the way to obtain the same gift from God. They said: *See, we have left all things and followed you.* We too follow the Lord, and we keep his feast by deeds rather than by words. ❦

We Are Soon Going to Share in the Passover

Saint Gregory Nazianzen, Bishop
[*From a Homily*]

We are soon going to share in the Passover, and although we still do so only in a symbolic way, the symbolism already has more clarity than it possessed in former times because, under the law, the Passover was, if I may dare to say so, only a symbol of a symbol. Before long, however, when the Word drinks the new wine with us in the kingdom of his Father, we shall be keeping the Passover in a yet more perfect way, and with deeper understanding. He will then reveal to us and make clear what he has so far only partially disclosed. For this wine, so familiar to us now, is eternally new.

It is for us to learn what this drinking is, and for him to teach us. He has to communicate this knowledge to his disciples, because teaching is food, even for the teacher.

So let us take our part in the Passover prescribed by the law, not in a literal way, but according to the teaching of the Gospel; not in an imperfect way, but perfectly; not only for a time, but eternally. Let us regard as our home the heavenly Jerusalem, not the earthly one; the city glorified by angels, not the one laid waste by armies. We are not required to sacrifice young bulls or rams, beasts with horns and hoofs that are more dead than alive and devoid of feeling; but instead, let us join the choirs of angels in offering God upon his heavenly altar a sacrifice of praise. We must now pass through the first veil and approach the second, turning our eyes toward the Holy of Holies. I will say more: we must sacrifice ourselves to God, each day and in everything we do, accepting all that happens to us for the sake of the Word, imitating his passion by our sufferings, and honoring his blood by shedding our own. We must be ready to be crucified.

If you are a Simon of Cyrene, take up your cross and follow Christ. If you are crucified beside him like one of the thieves, now, like the good thief, acknowledge your God. For your sake, and because of your sin, Christ himself was regarded as a sinner; for his sake, therefore, you must cease to sin. Worship him who was hung on the cross because of you, even if you are hanging there yourself. Derive some benefit from the very shame; purchase salvation with your death. Enter paradise with Jesus, and discover how far you have fallen. Contemplate the glories there, and leave the other scoffing thief to die outside in his blasphemy.

If you are a Joseph of Arimathea, go to the one who ordered his crucifixion, and ask for Christ's body. Make your own the expiation for the sins of the whole world. If you are a Nicodemus, like the man who worshipped God by night, bring spices and prepare Christ's body for burial. If you are one of the Marys, or Salome, or Joanna, weep in the early morning. Be the first to see the stone rolled back, and even the angels perhaps, and Jesus himself. ∽

THE MYSTERY OF OUR NEW LIFE IN CHRIST

Saint Gregory the Great, Pope

[*From the Moral Reflections on Job*]

Holy Job is a type of the Church. At one time he speaks for the body, at another for the head. As he speaks of its members he is suddenly caught up to speak in the name of their head. So it is here, where he says: *I have suffered this without sin on my hands, for my prayer to God was pure.*

Christ suffered without sin on his hands, for he committed no sin and deceit was not found on his lips. Yet he suffered the pain of the cross for our redemption. His prayer to God was pure, his alone out of all mankind for in the midst of his suffering he prayed for his persecutors: *Father, forgive them, for they do not know what they are doing.*

Is it possible to offer, or even to imagine, a purer kind of prayer than that which shows mercy to one's torturers by making intercession for them? It was thanks to this kind of prayer that the frenzied persecutors who shed the blood of our Redeemer drank it afterward in faith and proclaimed him to be the Son of God.

The text goes on fittingly to speak of Christ's blood: *Earth, do not cover over my blood, do not let my cry find a hiding place in you.* When man sinned, God had said: *Earth you are, and to earth you will return.* Earth does not cover over the blood of our Redeemer, for every sinner, as he drinks the blood that is the price of his redemption, offers praise and thanksgiving, and to the best of his power makes that blood known to all around him.

Earth has not hidden away his blood, for holy Church has preached in every corner of the world the mystery of its redemption.

Notice what follows: *Do not let my cry find a hiding place in you.* The blood that is drunk, the blood of redemption, is itself the cry of our Redeemer. Paul speaks of *the sprinkled blood that calls out more eloquently than Abel's.* Of Abel's blood Scripture had written: *The voice of your brother's blood cries out to me from the earth.* The blood of Jesus calls out more eloquently than Abel's, for the blood of Abel asked for the death of Cain the fratricide, while the blood of the Lord has asked for, and obtained, life for his persecutors.

If the sacrament of the Lord's passion is to work its effect in us, we must imitate what we receive and proclaim to mankind what we revere. The cry of the Lord finds a hiding place in us if our lips fail to speak of this, though our hearts believe in it. So that his cry may not lie concealed in us it remains for us all, each in his own measure, to make known to those around us the mystery of our new life in Christ. ✑

THE SPIRITUAL PASSOVER

From an Ancient Homily

The Passover we celebrate brings salvation to the whole human race beginning with the first man, who together with all others is saved and given life.

In an imperfect and transitory way, the types and images of the past prefigured the perfect and eternal reality which has now been revealed. The presence of what is represented makes the symbol obsolete: when the king appears in person no one pays reverence to his statue.

How far the symbol falls short of the reality is seen from the fact that the symbolic Passover celebrated the brief life of the firstborn of the Jews, whereas the real Passover celebrates the eternal life of all mankind. It is a small gain to escape death for a short time, only to die soon afterward; it is a very different thing to escape death altogether as we do through the sacrifice of Christ, our Passover.

Correctly understood, its very name shows why this is our greatest feast. It is called the Passover because, when he was striking down the firstborn, the destroying angel passed over the houses of the Hebrews, but it is even more true to say that he passes over us, for he does so once for all when we are raised up by Christ to eternal life.

If we think only of the true Passover and ask why it is that the time of the Passover and the salvation of the firstborn is taken to be the beginning of the year, the answer must surely be that the sacrifice of the true Passover is for us the beginning of eternal life. Because it revolves in cycles and never comes to an end, the year is a symbol of eternity.

Christ, the sacrifice that was offered for us, is the father of the world to come. He puts an end to our former life, and through the regenerating waters of baptism in which we imitate his death and resurrection, he gives us the beginning of a new life. The knowledge that Christ is the Passover lamb who was sacrificed for us should make us regard the moment of his immolation as the beginning of our own lives. As far as we are concerned, Christ's immolation on our behalf takes place when we become aware of this grace and understand the life conferred on us by this sacrifice. Having once understood it, we should enter upon this new life with all eagerness and never return to the old one, which is now at an end. As Scripture says: *We have died to sin — how then can we continue to live in it?* ❦

FIRSTBORN OF MANY BROTHERS

Blessed Isaac of Stella, Abbot
[*From a Sermon*]

Just as the head and body of a man form one single man, so the Son of the Virgin and those he has chosen to be his members form a single man and the one Son of Man. *Christ is whole and entire, head and body*, say the Scriptures, since all the members form one body, which with its head is one Son of Man, and he with the Son of God is one Son of God, who himself with God is one God. Therefore the whole body with its head is Son of Man, Son of God, and God. This is the explanation of the Lord's words: *Father, I desire that as you and I are one, so they may be one with us.*

And so, according to this well-known reading of Scripture, neither the body without the head, nor the head without the body, nor the head and body without God make the whole Christ. When all are united with God they become one God. The Son of God is one with God by nature; the Son of Man is one with him in his person; we, his body, are one with him sacramentally. Consequently those who by faith are spiritual members of Christ can truly say that they are what he is: the son of God and God himself. But what Christ is by his nature we are as his partners; what he is of himself in all fullness, we are as participants. Finally, what the Son of God is by generation, his members are by adoption, according to the text: *As sons you have received the Spirit of adoption, enabling you to cry, Abba, Father.*

Through his Spirit, he gave men the power to become sons of God, so that all those he has chosen might be taught by the firstborn among many brothers to say: *Our Father, who are in heaven.* Again he says elsewhere: *I ascend to my Father and to your Father.*

By the Spirit, from the womb of the Virgin, was born our head, the Son of Man; and by the same Spirit, in the waters of baptism, we are reborn as his body and as sons of God. And just as he was born without any sin, so we are reborn in the forgiveness of all our sins. As on the cross he bore the sum total of the whole body's sins in his own physical body, so he gave his members the grace of rebirth in order that no sin might be imputed to his mystical body. It is written: *Blessed is the man to whom the Lord imputes no sin.* The blessed man of this text is undoubtedly Christ, who forgives sins insofar as God is his head. Insofar as this man is the head of the body, no sin is forgiven him. But insofar as the body that belongs to this head consists of many members, sin is not imputed to it.

Just in himself, it is he who justifies himself. He alone is both Savior and saved. In his own body on the cross he bore what he had washed from his body by the waters of baptism. Bringing salvation through wood and through water, he is the Lamb of God who takes away the sins of the world which he took upon himself. Himself a priest, he offers himself as sacrifice to God, and he himself is God. Thus, through his own self, the Son is reconciled to himself as God, as well as to the Father and to the Holy Spirit. ❧

5

The Cross of Christ

THE CROSS OF CHRIST IS THE SOURCE OF ALL BLESSINGS, THE CAUSE OF ALL GRACES

Saint Leo the Great, Pope
[*From a Sermon*]

Our understanding, which is enlightened by the Spirit of truth, should receive with purity and freedom of heart the glory of the cross as it shines in heaven and on earth. It should see with inner vision the meaning of the Lord's words when he spoke of the imminence of his passion: *The hour has come for the Son of Man to be glorified.* Afterward he said: *Now my soul is troubled, and what am I to say? Father, save me from this hour. But it was for this that I came to this hour. Father, glorify your Son.* When the voice of the Father came from heaven, saying, *I have glorified him, and will glorify him again,* Jesus said in reply to those around him: *It was not for me that this voice spoke, but for you. Now is the judgment of the world, now will the prince of this world be cast out. And I, if I am lifted up from the earth, will draw all things to myself.*

How marvelous the power of the cross; how great beyond all telling the glory of the passion: here is the judgment-seat of the Lord, the condemnation of the world, the supremacy of Christ crucified.

Lord, you drew all things to yourself so that the devotion of all peoples everywhere might celebrate, in a sacrament made perfect and visible, what was carried out in the one temple of Judaea under obscure foreshadowings.

Now there is a more distinguished order of levites, a greater dignity for the rank of elders, a more sacred anointing for the priesthood, because your cross is the source of all blessings, the cause of all graces. Through the cross the faithful receive strength from weakness, glory from dishonor, life from death.

The different sacrifices of animals are no more: the one offering of your body and blood is the fulfillment of all the different sacrificial offerings, for you are the true *Lamb of God: you take away the sins of the world.* In yourself you bring to perfection all mysteries, so that, as there is one sacrifice in place of all other sacrificial offerings, there is also one kingdom gathered from all peoples.

Dearly beloved, let us then acknowledge what Saint Paul, the teacher of the nations, acknowledged so exultantly: *This is a saying worthy of trust, worthy of complete acceptance: Christ Jesus came into this world to save sinners.*

God's compassion for us is all the more wonderful because Christ died, not for the righteous or the holy but for the wicked and the sinful, and, though the divine nature could not be touched by the sting of death, he took to himself, through his birth as one of us, something he could offer on our behalf.

The power of his death once confronted our death. In the words of Hosea the prophet: *Death, I shall be your death; grave, I shall swallow you up.* By dying he submitted to the laws of the underworld; by rising again he destroyed them. He did away with the everlasting character of death so as to make death a thing of time, not of eternity. *As all die in Adam, so all will be brought to life in Christ.* ❧

THE CROSS OF CHRIST GIVES LIFE TO THE HUMAN RACE

Saint Ephrem, Deacon
[*From a Sermon*]

Death trampled our Lord underfoot, but he in his turn treated death as a highroad for his own feet. He submitted to it, enduring it willingly, because by this means he would be able to destroy death in spite of itself. Death had its own way when our Lord went out from Jerusalem carrying his cross; but when by a loud cry from that cross he summoned the dead from the underworld, death was powerless to prevent it.

Death slew him by means of the body which he had assumed, but that same body proved to be the weapon with which he conquered death. Concealed beneath the cloak of his manhood, his godhead engaged death in combat; but in slaying our Lord, death itself was slain.

It was able to kill natural human life, but was itself killed by the life that is above the nature of man.

Death could not devour our Lord unless he possessed a body, neither could hell swallow him up unless he bore our flesh; and so he came in search of a chariot in which to ride to the underworld. This chariot was the body which he received from the Virgin; in it he invaded death's fortress, broke open its strong room and scattered all its treasure.

At length he came upon Eve, the mother of all the living. She was the vineyard whose enclosure her own hands had enabled death to violate, so that she could taste its fruit; thus the mother of all the living became the source of death for every living creature. But in her stead Mary grew up, a new vine in place of the old. Christ, the new life, dwelt within her. When death, with its customary impudence, came foraging for her mortal fruit, it encountered its own destruction in the hidden life that fruit contained. All unsuspecting, it swallowed him up, and in so doing released life itself and set free a multitude of men.

He who was also the carpenter's glorious son set up his cross above death's all-consuming jaws, and led the human race into the dwelling place of life. Since a tree had brought about the downfall of mankind, it was upon a tree that mankind crossed over to the realm of life. Bitter was the branch that had once been grafted upon that ancient tree, but sweet the young shoot that has now been grafted in, the shoot in which we are meant to recognize the Lord whom no creature can resist.

We give glory to you, Lord, who raised up your cross to span the jaws of death like a bridge by which souls might pass from the region of the dead to the land of the living. We give glory to you who put on the body of a single mortal man and made it the source of life for every other mortal man. You are incontestably alive. Your murderers sowed your living body in the earth as farmers sow grain, but it sprang up and yielded an abundant harvest of men raised from the dead.

Come then, my brothers and sisters, let us offer our Lord the great and all-embracing sacrifice of our love, pouring out our treasury of hymns and prayers before him who offered his cross in sacrifice to God for the enrichment of us all.

THE PRECIOUS AND LIFE-GIVING
CROSS OF CHRIST

Saint Theodore the Studite
[*From a Sermon*]

How precious the gift of the cross, how splendid to contemplate! In the cross there is no mingling of good and evil, as in the tree of paradise: it is wholly beautiful to behold and good to taste. The fruit of this tree is not death but life, not darkness but light. This tree does not cast us out of paradise, but opens the way for our return.

This was the tree on which Christ, like a king on a chariot, destroyed the devil, the Lord of death, and freed the human race from his tyranny. This was the tree upon which the Lord, like a brave warrior wounded in hands, feet and side, healed the wounds of sin that the evil serpent had inflicted on our nature. A tree once caused our death, but now a tree brings life. Once deceived by a tree, we have now repelled the cunning serpent by a tree. What an astonishing transformation! That death should become life, that decay should become immortality, that shame should become glory! Well might the holy Apostle exclaim: *Far be it from me to glory except in the cross of our Lord Jesus Christ, by which the world has been crucified to me, and I to the world!* The supreme wisdom that flowered on the cross has shown the folly of worldly wisdom's pride. The knowledge of all good, which is the fruit of the cross, has cut away the shoots of wickedness.

The wonders accomplished through this tree were foreshadowed clearly even by the mere types and figures that existed in the past. Meditate on these, if you are eager to learn. Was it not the wood of a tree that enabled Noah, at God's command, to escape the destruction of the flood together with his sons, his wife, his sons' wives and every kind of animal? And surely the rod of Moses prefigured the cross when it changed water into blood, swallowed up the false serpents of Pharaoh's magicians, divided the sea at one stroke and then restored the waters to their normal course, drowning the enemy and saving God's own people? Aaron's rod, which blossomed in one day in proof of his true priesthood, was another figure of the cross, and did not Abraham foreshadow the cross when he bound his son Isaac and placed him on the pile of wood?

By the cross death was slain and Adam was restored to life. The cross is the glory of all the apostles, the crown of the martyrs, the sanctification of the saints. By the cross we put on Christ and cast aside our former self. By the cross we, the sheep of Christ, have been gathered into one flock, destined for the sheepfolds of heaven. ❧

LET US TOO GLORY IN THE CROSS OF THE LORD

Saint Augustine, Bishop
[*From a Sermon*]

The passion of our Lord and Savior Jesus Christ is the hope of glory and a lesson in patience.

What may not the hearts of believers promise themselves as the gift of God's grace, when for their sake God's only Son, co-eternal with the Father, was not content only to be born as man from human stock but even died at the hands of the men he had created?

It is a great thing that we are promised by the Lord; but far greater is what has already been done for us, and which we now commemorate. Where were the sinners, what were they, when Christ died for them? When Christ has already given us the gift of his death, who is to doubt that he will give the saints the gift of his own life? Why does our human frailty hesitate to believe that mankind will one day live with God?

Who is Christ if not the Word of God: *in the beginning was the Word, and the Word was with God, and the Word was God?* This Word of God *was made flesh and dwelt among us.* He had no power of himself to die for us: he had to take from us our mortal flesh. This was the way in which, though immortal, he was able to die; the way in which he chose to give life to mortal men: he would first share with us, and then enable us to share with him. Of ourselves we had no power to live, nor did he of himself have the power to die.

Accordingly, he effected a wonderful exchange with us, through mutual sharing: we gave him the power to die, he will give us the power to live.

The death of the Lord our God should not be a cause of shame for us; rather, it should be our greatest hope, our greatest glory. In taking upon himself the death that he found in us, he has most faithfully promised to give us life in him, such as we cannot have of ourselves.

He loved us so much that, sinless himself, he suffered for us sinners the punishment we deserved for our sins. How then can he fail to give us the reward we deserve for our righteousness, for he is the source of righteousness? How can he, whose promises are true, fail to reward the saints when he bore the punishment of sinners, though without sin himself?

Brethren, let us then fearlessly acknowledge, and even openly proclaim, that Christ was crucified for us; let us confess it, not in fear but in joy, not in shame but in glory.

The apostle Paul saw Christ, and extolled his claim to glory. He had many great and inspired things to say about Christ, but he did not say that he boasted in Christ's wonderful works: in creating the world, since he was God with the Father, or in ruling the world, through he was also a man like us. Rather, he said: *Let me not boast except in the cross of our Lord Jesus Christ.*

THE PASSION OF THE WHOLE BODY OF CHRIST

Saint Augustine, Bishop
[*From a Commentary on the Psalms*]

Lord, I have cried to you, hear me. This is a prayer we can all say. This is not my prayer, but that of the whole Christ. Rather, it is said in the name of his body. When Christ was on earth he prayed in his human nature, and prayed to the Father in the name of his body, and when he prayed drops of blood flowed from his whole body. So it is written in the Gospel: *Jesus prayed with earnest prayer, and sweated blood.* What is this blood streaming from his whole body but the martyrdom of the whole Church?

Lord, I have cried to you, hear me; listen to the sound of my prayer, when I call upon you. Did you imagine that crying was over when you said: *I have cried to you?* You have cried out, but do not as yet feel free from care. If anguish is at an end, crying is at an end; but if the Church, the body of Christ, must suffer anguish until the end of time, it must not say only: *I have cried to you, hear me;* it must also say: *Listen to the sound of my prayer, when I call upon you.*

Let my prayer rise like incense in your sight; let the raising of my hands be an evening sacrifice.

This is generally understood of Christ, the head, as every Christian acknowledges. When day was fading into evening, the Lord laid down his life on the cross, to take it up again; he did not lose his life against his will. Here, too, we are symbolized. What part of him hung on the cross if not the part he had received from us? How could God the Father ever cast off and abandon his only Son, who is indeed one God with him? Yet Christ, nailing our weakness to the cross (where, as the Apostle says: *Our old nature was nailed to the cross with him*), cried out with the very voice of our humanity: *My God, my God, why have you forsaken me?*

The evening sacrifice is then the passion of the Lord, the cross of the Lord, the oblation of the victim that brings salvation, the holocaust acceptable to God. In his resurrection he made this evening sacrifice a morning sacrifice. Prayer offered in holiness from a faithful heart rises like incense from a holy altar. Nothing is more fragrant than the fragrance of the Lord. May all who believe share in this fragrance.

Therefore, *our old nature*, in the words of the Apostle, *was nailed to the cross with him, in order*, as he says, *to destroy our sinful body, so that we may be slaves to sin no longer.* ❧

CONTEMPLATING THE LORD'S PASSION

Saint Leo the Great, Pope

[*From a Sermon*]

True reverence for the Lord's passion means fixing the eyes of our heart on Jesus crucified and recognizing in him our own humanity.

The earth—our earthly nature—should tremble at the suffering of its Redeemer. The rocks—the hearts of unbelievers—should burst asunder. The dead, imprisoned in the tombs of their mortality, should come forth, the massive stones now ripped apart. Foreshadowings of the future resurrection should appear in the holy city, the Church of God: what is to happen to our bodies should now take place in our hearts.

No one, however weak, is denied a share in the victory of the cross. No one is beyond the help of the prayer of Christ. His prayer brought benefit to the multitude that raged against him. How much more does it bring to those who turn to him in repentance.

Ignorance has been destroyed, obstinacy has been overcome. The sacred blood of Christ has quenched the flaming sword that barred access to the tree of life. The age-old night of sin has given place to the true light.

The Christian people are invited to share the riches of paradise. All who have been reborn have the way open before them to return to their native land, from which they had been exiled. Unless indeed they close off for themselves the path that could be opened before the faith of a thief.

The business of this life should not preoccupy us with its anxiety and pride, so that we no longer strive with all the love of our heart to be like our Redeemer, and to follow his example. Everything that he did or suffered was for our salvation: he wanted his body to share the goodness of its head.

First of all, in taking our human nature while remaining God, so that *the Word became man,* he left no member of the human race, the unbeliever excepted, without a share in his mercy. Who does not share a common nature with Christ if he has welcomed Christ, who took our nature, and is reborn in the Spirit through whom Christ was conceived?

Again, who cannot recognize in Christ his own infirmities? Who would not recognize that Christ's eating and sleeping, his sadness and his shedding tears of love are marks of the nature of a slave?

It was this nature of a slave that had to be healed of its ancient wounds and cleansed of the defilement of sin. For that reason the only-begotten Son of God became also the son of man. He was to have both the reality of a human nature and the fullness of the godhead.

The body that lay lifeless in the tomb is ours. The body that rose again on the third day is ours. The body that ascended above all the heights of heaven to the right hand of the Father's glory is ours. If then we walk in the way of his commandments, and are not ashamed to acknowledge the price he paid for our salvation in a lowly body, we too are to rise to share his glory. The promise he made will be fulfilled in the sight of all: *Whoever acknowledges me before men, I too will acknowledge him before my Father who is in heaven.*

6

The Risen Christ

CHRIST IS THE DAY

Saint Maximus of Turin, Bishop
[*From a Sermon*]

Christ is risen! He has burst open the gates of hell and let the dead go free; he has renewed the earth through the members of his Church now born again in baptism, and has made it blossom afresh with men brought back to life. His Holy Spirit has unlocked the doors of heaven, which stand wide open to receive those who rise up from the earth. Because of Christ's resurrection the thief ascends to paradise, the bodies of the blessed enter the holy city, and the dead are restored to the company of the living. There is an upward movement in the whole of creation, each element raising itself to something higher. We see hell restoring its victims to the upper regions, earth sending its buried dead to heaven, and heaven presenting the new arrivals to the Lord. In one and the same movement, our Savior's passion raises men from the depths, lifts them up from the earth, and sets them in the heights.

Christ is risen. His rising brings life to the dead, forgiveness to sinners, and glory to the saints. And so David the prophet summons all creation to join in celebrating the Easter festival: *Rejoice and be glad*, he cries, *on this day which the Lord has made*.

The light of Christ is an endless day that knows no night. Christ is this day, says the Apostle; such is the meaning of his words: *Night is almost over; day is at hand*. He tells us that night is almost over, not that it is about to fall. By this we are meant to understand that the coming of Christ's light puts Satan's darkness to flight, leaving no place for any shadow of sin. His everlasting radiance dispels the dark clouds of the past and checks the hidden growth of vice. The Son is that day to whom the day, which is the Father, communicates the mystery of his divinity. He is the day who says through the mouth of Solomon: *I have caused an unfailing light to rise in heaven*. And as in heaven no night can follow day, so no sin can overshadow the justice of Christ. The celestial day is perpetually bright and shining with brilliant light; clouds can never darken its skies. In the same way, the light of Christ is eternally glowing with luminous radiance and can never be extinguished by the darkness of sin. This is why John the evangelist says: *The light shines in the darkness, and the darkness has never been able to overpower it*.

And so, my brothers, each of us ought surely to rejoice on this holy day. Let no one, conscious of his sinfulness, withdraw from our common celebration, nor let anyone be kept away from our public prayer by the burden of his guilt. Sinner he may indeed be, but he must not despair of pardon on this day which is so highly privileged; for if a thief could receive the grace of paradise, how could a Christian be refused forgiveness? ❧

CHRIST THE SOURCE
OF RESURRECTION AND LIFE

[From an Easter Homily by an Ancient Author]

Saint Paul rejoices in the knowledge that spiritual health has been restored to the human race. *Death entered the world through Adam,* he explains, *but life has been given back to the world through Christ.* Again he says: *The first man, being from the earth, is earthly by nature; the second man is from heaven and is heavenly. As we have borne the image of the earthly man,* the image of human nature grown old in sin, *so let us bear the image of the heavenly man:* human nature raised up, redeemed, restored and purified in Christ. We must hold fast to the salvation we have received. *Christ was the firstfruits,* says the Apostle; he is the source of resurrection and life. *Those who belong to Christ will follow him.* Modeling their lives on his purity, they will be secure in the hope of his resurrection and of enjoying with him the glory promised in heaven. Our Lord himself said so in the gospel: *Whoever follows me will not perish, but will pass from death to life.*

Thus the passion of our Savior is the salvation of mankind. The reason why he desired to die for us was that he wanted us who believe in him to live for ever. In the fullness of time it was his will to become what we are, so that we might inherit the eternity he promised and live with him for ever.

Here, then, is the grace conferred by these heavenly mysteries, the gift which Easter brings, the most longed-for feast of the year; here are the beginnings of creatures newly formed: children born from the life-giving font of holy Church, born anew with the simplicity of little ones, and crying out with the evidence of a clean conscience. Chaste fathers and inviolate mothers accompany this new family, countless in number, born to new life through faith. As they emerge from the grace-giving womb of the font, a blaze of candles burns brightly beneath the tree of faith. The Easter festival brings the grace of holiness from heaven to men. Through the repeated celebration of the sacred mysteries they receive the spiritual nourishment of the sacraments. Fostered at the very heart of holy church, the fellowship of one community worships the one God, adoring the triple name of his essential holiness, and together with the prophet sings the psalm which belongs to this yearly festival: *This is the day the Lord has made; let us rejoice and be glad.* And what is this day? It is the Lord Jesus Christ himself, the author of light, who brings the sunrise and the beginning of life, saying of himself: *I am the light of day; whoever walks in daylight does not stumble.*

That is to say, whoever follows Christ in all things will come by this path to the throne of eternal light.

Such was the prayer Christ made to the Father while he was still on earth: *Father, I desire that where I am they also may be, those who have come to believe in me; and that as you are in me and I in you, so they may abide in us.* ⌘

THE EASTER PRAISE OF CHRIST

Saint Melito of Sardis, Bishop
[*From an Easter Homily*]

We should understand, beloved, that the paschal mystery is at once old and new, transitory and eternal, corruptible and incorruptible, mortal and immortal. In terms of the Law it is old, in terms of the Word it is new. In its figure it is passing, in its grace it is eternal. It is corruptible in the sacrifice of the lamb, incorruptible in the eternal life of the Lord. It is mortal in his burial in the earth, immortal in his resurrection from the dead.

The Law indeed is old, but the Word is new. The type is transitory, but grace is eternal. The lamb was corruptible, but the Lord is incorruptible. He was slain as a lamb; he rose again as God. *He was led like a sheep to the slaughter*, yet he was not a sheep. He was silent as a lamb, yet he was not a lamb. The type has passed away; the reality has come. The lamb gives place to

God, the sheep gives place to a man, and the man is Christ, who fills the whole of creation. The sacrifice of the lamb, the celebration of the Passover, and the prescriptions of the Law have been fulfilled in Jesus Christ. Under the old Law, and still more under the new dispensation, everything pointed toward him.

Both the Law and the Word came forth from Zion and Jerusalem, but now the Law has given place to the Word, the old to the new. The commandment has become grace, the type a reality. The lamb has become a Son, the sheep a man, and man, God.

The Lord, though he was God, became man. He suffered for the sake of those who suffer, he was bound for those in bonds, condemned for the guilty, buried for those who lie in the grave; but he rose from the dead, and cried aloud: *Who will contend with me? Let him confront me.* I have freed the condemned, brought the dead back to life, raised men from their graves. Who has anything to say against me? I, he said, am the Christ; I have destroyed death, triumphed over the enemy, trampled hell underfoot, bound the strong one, and taken men up to the heights of heaven: I am the Christ.

Come, then, all you nations of men, receive forgiveness for the sins that defile you. I am your forgiveness. I am the Passover that brings salvation. I am the lamb who was immolated for you. I am your ransom, your life, your resurrection, your light, I am your salvation and your king. I will bring you to the heights of heaven. With my own right hand I will raise you up, and I will show you the eternal Father.

GOD HAS RECONCILED US TO HIMSELF THROUGH CHRIST AND GIVEN US THE MINISTRY OF RECONCILIATION

Saint Cyril of Alexandria, Bishop
[*From the Commentary on the
Second Letter to the Corinthians*]

Those who have a sure hope, guaranteed by the Spirit, that they will rise again lay hold of what lies in the future as though it were already present. They say: Outward appearances will no longer be our standard in judging other men. Our lives are all controlled by the Spirit now, and are not confined to this physical world that is subject to corruption. The light of the Only-begotten has shone on us, and we have been transformed into the Word, the source of all life. While sin was still our master, the bonds of death had a firm hold on us, but now that the righteousness of Christ has found a place in our hearts we have freed ourselves from our former condition of corruptibility.

This means that none of us lives in the flesh any more, at least not in so far as living in the flesh means being subject to the weaknesses of the flesh, which include corruptibility. *Once we thought of Christ as being in the flesh, but we do not do so any longer,* says Saint Paul. By this he meant that the Word became flesh and dwelt among us; he suffered death in the flesh in order to give all men life. It was in this flesh that we knew him before, but we do so no longer. Even though he remains in the flesh, since he came to life again on the third day and is now with his Father in heaven, we know that he has passed beyond the life of the flesh; for *having died once, he will never die again, death has no power over him any more. His death was a death to sin, which he died once for all; his life is life with God.*

Since Christ has in this way become the source of life for us, we who follow in his footsteps must not think of ourselves as living in the flesh any longer, but as having passed beyond it. Saint Paul's saying is absolutely true that *when anyone is in Christ he becomes a completely different person; his old life is over and a new life has begun.* We have been justified by our faith in Christ and the power of the curse has been broken. Christ's coming to life again for our sake has put an end to the sovereignty of death. We have come to know the true God and to worship him in spirit and in truth, through the Son, our mediator, who sends down upon the world the Father's blessings.

And so Saint Paul shows deep insight when he says: *This is all God's doing: it is he who has reconciled us to himself through Christ.* For the mystery of the incarnation and the renewal it accomplished could not have taken place without the Father's will. Through Christ we have gained access to the Father, for as Christ himself says, no one comes to the Father except through him. *This is all God's doing,* then. *It is he who has reconciled us to himself through Christ, and who has given us the ministry of reconciliation.* ♋

THE FIRSTBORN OF THE NEW CREATION

Saint Gregory of Nyssa, Bishop
[*From a Sermon*]

The reign of life has begun, the tyranny of death is ended. A new birth has taken place, a new life has come, a new order of existence has appeared, our very nature has been transformed! This birth is not brought about *by human generation, by the will of man, or by the desire of the flesh, but by God.*

If you wonder how, I will explain in clear language. Faith is the womb that conceives this new life, baptism the rebirth by which it is brought forth into the light of day. The Church is its nurse; her teachings are its milk, the bread from heaven is its food. It is brought to maturity by the practice of virtue; it is wedded to wisdom; it gives birth to hope. Its home is the kingdom; its rich inheritance the joys of paradise; its end, not death, but the blessed and everlasting life prepared for those who are worthy.

This is the day the Lord has made — a day far different from those made when the world was first created and which are measured by the passage of time. This is the beginning of a new creation. On this day, as the prophet says, God makes a new heaven and a new earth. What is this new heaven? you may ask. It is the firmament of our faith in Christ. What is this new earth? A good heart, a heart like the earth, which drinks up the rain that falls on it and yields a rich harvest.

In this new creation, purity of life is the sun, the virtues are the stars, transparent goodness is the air, and *the depths of the riches of wisdom and knowledge*, the sea. Sound doctrine, the divine teachings are the grass and plants that feed God's flock, the people whom he shepherds; the keeping of the commandments is the fruit borne by the trees.

On this day is created the true man, the man made in the image and likeness of God. For *this day the Lord has made* is the beginning of this new world. Of this day the prophet says that it is not like other days, nor is this night like other nights. But still we have not spoken of the greatest gift it has brought us. This day destroyed the pangs of death and brought to birth the firstborn of the dead.

I ascend to my Father and to your Father, to my God and to your God. O what wonderful good news! He who for our sake became like us in order to make us his brothers, now presents to his true Father his own humanity in order to draw all his kindred up after him. ❧

THE DAYS BETWEEN THE RESURRECTION AND ASCENSION OF OUR LORD

Saint Leo the Great, Pope
[*From a Sermon*]

Beloved, the days which passed between the Lord's resurrection and his ascension were by no means uneventful; during them great sacramental mysteries were confirmed, great truths revealed. In those days the fear of death with all its horrors was taken away, and the immortality of both body and soul affirmed. It was then that the Lord breathed on all his apostles and filled them with the Holy Spirit; and after giving the keys of the kingdom to blessed Peter, whom he had chosen and set above all the others, he entrusted him with the care of his flock.

During these days the Lord joined two of his disciples as their companion on the road, and by chiding them for their timidity and hesitant fears he swept away all the clouds of our uncertainty. Their lukewarm hearts were fired by the light of faith and began to burn within them as the Lord opened up the Scriptures. And as they shared their meal with him, their eyes were opened in the breaking of bread, opened far more happily to the sight of their own glorified humanity than were the eyes of our first parents to the shame of their sin.

Throughout the whole period between the resurrection and ascension, God's providence was at work to instill this one lesson into the hearts of the disciples, to set this one truth before their eyes, that our Lord Jesus Christ, who was truly born, truly suffered and truly died, should be recognized as truly risen from the dead. The blessed apostles together with all the others had been intimidated by the catastrophe of the cross, and their faith in the resurrection had been uncertain; but now they were so strengthened by the evident truth that when their Lord ascended into heaven, far from feeling any sadness, they were filled with great joy.

Indeed that blessed company had a great and inexpressible cause for joy when it saw man's nature rising above the dignity of the whole heavenly creation, above the ranks of angels, above the exalted status of archangels. Nor would there be any limit to its upward course until humanity was admitted to a seat at the right hand of the eternal Father, to be enthroned at last in the glory of him to whose nature it was wedded in the person of the Son. ❧

No One Has Ever Ascended into Heaven Except the One Who Descended From Heaven

Saint Augustine, Bishop
[*From a Sermon*]

Today our Lord Jesus Christ ascended into heaven; let our hearts ascend with him. Listen to the words of the Apostle: *If you have risen with Christ, set your hearts on the things that are above where Christ is, seated at the right hand of God; seek the things that are above, not the things that are on earth.* For just as he remained with us even after his ascension, so we too are already in heaven with him, even though what is promised us has not yet been fulfilled in our bodies.

Christ is now exalted above the heavens, but he still suffers on earth all the pain that we, the members of his body, have to bear. He showed this when he cried out from above: *Saul, Saul, why do you persecute me?* and when he said: *I was hungry and you gave me food.*

Why do we on earth not strive to find rest with him in heaven even now, through the faith, hope and love that unites us to him? While in heaven he is also with us; and we while on earth are with him. He is here with us by his divinity, his power and his love. We cannot be in heaven, as he is on earth, by divinity, but in him, we can be there by love.

He did not leave heaven when he came down to us; nor did he withdraw from us when he went up again into heaven. The fact that he was in heaven even while he was on earth is borne out by his own statement: *No one has ever ascended into heaven except the one who descended from heaven, the Son of Man, who is in heaven.*

These words are explained by our oneness with Christ, for he is our head and we are his body. No one ascended into heaven except Christ because we also are Christ: he is the Son of Man by his union with us, and we by our union with him are sons of God. So the Apostle says: *Just as the human body, which has many members, is a unity, because all the different members make one body, so is it also with Christ.* He too has many members, but one body.

Out of compassion for us he descended from heaven, and although he ascended alone, we also ascend, because we are in him by grace. Thus, no one but Christ descended and no one but Christ ascended; not because there is no distinction between the head and the body, but because the body as a unity cannot be separated from the head. ✎

Our Faith is Increased by
the Lord's Ascension

Saint Leo the Great, Pope
[*From a Sermon*]

At Easter, beloved brethren, it was the Lord's resurrection which was the cause of our joy; our present rejoicing is on account of his ascension into heaven. With all due solemnity we are commemorating that day on which our poor human nature was carried up, in Christ, above all the hosts of heaven, above all the ranks of angels, beyond the highest heavenly powers to the very throne of God the Father. It is upon this ordered structure of divine acts that we have been firmly established, so that the grace of God may show itself still more marvelous when, in spite of the withdrawal from men's sight of everything that is rightly felt to command their reverence, faith does not fail, hope is not shaken, charity does not grow cold.

For such is the power of great minds, such the light of truly believing souls, that they put unhesitating faith in what is not seen with the bodily eye; they fix their desires on what is beyond sight. Such fidelity could never be born in our hearts, nor could anyone be justified by faith, if our salvation lay only in what was visible.

And so our Redeemer's visible presence has passed into the sacraments. Our faith is nobler and stronger because sight has been replaced by a doctrine whose authority is accepted by believing hearts, enlightened from on high. This faith was increased by the Lord's ascension and strengthened by the gift of the Spirit; it would remain unshaken by fetters and imprisonment, exile and hunger, fire and ravening beasts, and the most refined tortures ever devised by brutal persecutors. Throughout the world women no less than men, tender girls as well as boys, have given their life's blood in the struggle for this faith. It is a faith that has driven out devils, healed the sick and raised the dead.

Even the blessed apostles, though they had been strengthened by so many miracles and instructed by so much teaching, took fright at the cruel suffering of the Lord's passion and could not accept his resurrection without hesitation. Yet they made such progress through his ascension that they now found joy in what had terrified them before. They were able to fix their minds on Christ's divinity as he sat at the right hand of his Father, since what was presented to their bodily eyes no longer hindered them from turning all their attention to the realization that he had not left his Father when he came down to earth, nor had he abandoned his disciples when he ascended into heaven.

The truth is that the Son of Man was revealed as Son of God in a more perfect and transcendent way once he had entered into his Father's glory; he now began to be indescribably more present in his divinity to those from whom he was further removed in his humanity. A more mature faith enabled their minds to stretch upward to the Son in his equality with the Father; it no longer needed contact with Christ's tangible body, in which as man he is inferior to the Father. For while his glorified body retained the same nature, the faith of those who believed in him was now summoned to heights where, as the Father's equal, the only-begotten Son is reached not by physical handling but by spiritual discernment. ❧

The Eucharist

THE EUCHARIST IS THE LORD'S PASSOVER

Saint Gaudentius of Brescia, Bishop
[*From a Treatise*]

One man has died for all, and now in every church in the mystery of bread and wine he heals those for whom he is offered in sacrifice, giving life to those who believe and holiness to those who consecrate the offering. This is the flesh of the Lamb; this is his blood. The bread that came down from heaven declared: *The bread that I will give is my flesh for the life of the world*. It is significant, too, that his blood should be given to us in the form of wine, for his own words in the gospel, *I am the true vine*, imply clearly enough that whenever wine is offered as a representation of Christ's passion, it is his blood. This means that it was of Christ that the blessed patriarch Jacob prophesied when he said: *He will wash his tunic in wine and his cloak in the blood of the grape*. The tunic was our flesh, which Christ was to put on like a garment and which he was to wash in his own blood.

Creator and Lord of all things, whatever their nature, he brought forth bread from the earth and changed it into his own body. Not only had he the power to do this, but he had promised it; and, as he had changed water into wine, he also changed wine into his own blood. *It is the Lord's Passover*, Scripture tells us, that is, the Lord's passing. We are no longer to look upon the bread and wine as earthly substances. They have become heavenly, because Christ has passed into them and changed them into his body and blood. What you receive is the body of him who is the heavenly bread, and the blood of him who is the sacred vine; for when he offered his disciples the consecrated bread and wine, he said: *This is my body, this is my blood.* We have put our trust in him. I urge you to have faith in him; truth can never deceive.

When Christ told the crowds that they must eat his flesh and drink his blood, they were horrified and began to murmur among themselves: *This teaching is too hard; who can be expected to listen to it?* As I have already told you, thoughts such as these must be banished. The Lord himself used heavenly fire to drive them away by going on to declare: *It is the spirit that gives life; the flesh is of no avail. The words that I have spoken to you are spirit and life.* ❧

THE UNITY OF THE FAITHFUL IN GOD THROUGH THE INCARNATION OF THE WORD AND THE SACRAMENT OF THE EUCHARIST

Saint Hilary, Bishop

[*From a Treatise "On the Trinity"*]

We believe that the Word became flesh and that we receive his flesh in the Lord's Supper. How then can we fail to believe that he really dwells within us? When he became man, he actually clothed himself in our flesh, uniting it to himself for ever. In the sacrament of his body he actually gives us his own flesh, which he has united to his divinity. This is why we are all one, because the Father is in Christ, and Christ is in us. He is in us through his flesh and we are in him. With him we form a unity which is in God.

The manner of our indwelling in him through the sacrament of his body and blood is evident from the Lord's own words: *This world will see me no longer but you shall see me. Because I live you shall live also, for I am in my Father, you are in me, and I am in you.* If it had been a question of a mere unity of will, why should he have given us this explanation of the steps by which it is achieved? He is in the Father by reason of his divine nature, we are in him by reason of his human birth, and he is in us through the mystery of the sacraments. This, surely, is what he wished us to believe; this is how he wanted us to understand the perfect unity that is achieved through our Mediator, who lives in the Father while we live in him, and who, while living in the Father, lives also in us. This is how we attain to unity with the Father. Christ is in very truth in the Father by his eternal generation; we are in very truth in Christ, and he likewise is in us.

Christ himself bore witness to the reality of this unity when he said: *He who eats my flesh and drinks my blood lives in me and I in him.* No one will be in Christ unless Christ himself has been in him; Christ will take to himself only the flesh of those who have received his flesh.

He had already explained the mystery of this perfect unity when he said: *As the living Father sent me and I draw life from the Father, so he who eats my flesh will draw life from me.* We draw life from his flesh just as he draws life from the Father. Such comparisons aid our understanding, since we can grasp a point more easily when we have an analogy. And the point is that Christ is the wellspring of our life. Since we who are in the flesh have Christ dwelling in us through his flesh, we shall draw life from him in the same way as he draws life from the Father. ❧

THE EUCHARIST, PLEDGE OF OUR RESURRECTION

Saint Irenaeus, Bishop
[*From the Treatise "Against Heresies"*]

If our flesh is not saved, then the Lord has not redeemed us with his blood, the eucharistic chalice does not make us sharers in his blood, and the bread we break does not make us sharers in his body. There can be no blood without veins, flesh and the rest of the human substance, and this the Word of God actually became: it was with his own blood that he redeemed us. As the Apostle says: *In him, through his blood, we have been redeemed, our sins have been forgiven.*

We are his members and we are nourished by creation, which is his gift to us, for it is he who causes the sun to rise and the rain to fall. He declared that the chalice, which comes from his creation, was his blood, and he makes it the nourishment of our blood. He affirmed that the bread, which comes from his creation, was his body, and he makes it the nourishment of our body. When the chalice we mix and the bread we bake receive the word of God, the eucharistic elements become the body and blood of Christ, by which our bodies live and grow. How then can it be said that flesh belonging to the Lord's own body and nourished by his body and blood is incapable of receiving God's gift of eternal life? Saint Paul says in his letter to the Ephesians that *we are members of his body*, of his flesh and bones.

He is not speaking of some spiritual and incorporeal kind of man, *for spirits do not have flesh and bones*. He is speaking of a real human body composed of flesh, sinews and bones, nourished by the chalice of Christ's blood and receiving growth from the bread which is his body.

The slip of a vine planted in the ground bears fruit at the proper time. The grain of wheat falls into the ground and decays only to be raised up again and multiplied by the Spirit of God who sustains all things. The Wisdom of God places these things at the service of man and when they receive God's word they become the eucharist, which is the body and blood of Christ. In the same way our bodies, which have been nourished by the eucharist, will be buried in the earth and will decay, but they will rise again at the appointed time, for the Word of God will raise them up to the glory of God the Father. Then the Father will clothe our mortal nature in immortality and freely endow our corruptible nature with incorruptibility, for God's power is shown most perfectly in weakness. ❧

THE CELEBRATION OF THE EUCHARIST

Saint Justin Martyr

[From the First Apology in Defense of the Christians]

No one may share the eucharist with us unless he believes that what we teach is true, unless he is washed in the regenerating waters of baptism for the remission of his sins, and unless he lives in accordance with the principles given us by Christ.

We do not consume the eucharistic bread and wine as if it were ordinary food and drink, for we have been taught that as Jesus Christ our Savior became a man of flesh and blood by the power of the Word of God, so also the food that our flesh and blood assimilates for its nourishment becomes the flesh and blood of the incarnate Jesus by the power of his own words contained in the prayer of thanksgiving.

The apostles, in their recollections, which are called gospels, handed down to us what Jesus commanded them to do. They tell us that he took bread, gave thanks and said: *Do this in memory of me. This is my body.* In the same way he took the cup, he gave thanks and said: *This is my blood.* The Lord gave this command to them alone. Ever since then we have constantly reminded one another of these things. The rich among us help the poor and we are always united. For all that we receive we praise the Creator of the universe through his Son Jesus Christ and through the Holy Spirit.

On Sunday we have a common assembly of all our members, whether they live in the city or in the outlying districts. The recollections of the apostles or the writings of the prophets are read, as long as there is time. When the reader has finished, the president of the assembly speaks to us; he urges everyone to imitate the examples of virtue we have heard in the readings. Then we all stand up together and pray.

On the conclusion of our prayer, bread and wine and water are brought forward. The president offers prayers and gives thanks to the best of his ability, and the people give their assent by saying, "Amen." The eucharist is distributed, everyone present communicates, and the deacons take it to those who are absent.

The wealthy, if they wish, may make a contribution, and they themselves decide the amount. The collection is placed in the custody of the president, who uses it to help the orphans and widows and all who for any reason are in distress, whether because they are sick, in prison, or away from home. In a word, he takes care of all who are in need.

We hold our common assembly on Sunday because it is the first day of the week, the day on which God put darkness and chaos to flight and created the world, and because on that same day our savior Jesus Christ rose from the dead. For he was crucified on Friday and on Sunday he appeared to his apostles and disciples and taught them the things that we have passed on for your consideration.

THE INHERITANCE OF THE NEW COVENANT

Saint Gaudentius of Brescia, Bishop
[*From a Sermon*]

The heavenly sacrifice, instituted by Christ, is the most gracious legacy of his new covenant. On the night he was delivered up to be crucified he left us this gift as a pledge of his abiding presence.

This sacrifice is our sustenance on life's journey; by it we are nourished and supported along the road of life until we depart from this world and make our way to the Lord. For this reason he addressed these words to us: *Unless you eat my flesh and drink my blood, you will not have life in you.*

It was the Lord's will that his gifts should remain with us, and that we who have been redeemed by his precious blood should constantly be sanctified according to the pattern of his own passion. And so he commanded those faithful disciples of his whom he made the first priests of his Church to enact these mysteries of eternal life continuously. All priests throughout the churches of the world must celebrate these mysteries until Christ comes again from heaven. Therefore let us all, priests and people alike, be faithful to this everlasting memorial of our redemption. Daily it is before our eyes as a representation of the passion of Christ. We hold it in our hands, we receive it in our mouths, and we accept it in our hearts.

It is appropriate that we should receive the body of Christ in the form of bread, because, as there are many grains of wheat in the flour from which bread is made by mixing it with water and baking it with fire, so also we know that many members make up the one body of Christ which is brought to maturity by the fire of the Holy Spirit. Christ was born of the Holy Spirit, and since it was fitting that he should fulfill all justice, he entered into the waters of baptism to sanctify them. When he left the Jordan he was filled with the Holy Spirit who had descended upon him in the form of a dove. As the evangelist tells us: *Jesus, full of the Holy Spirit, returned from the Jordan*.

Similarly, the wine of Christ's blood, drawn from the many grapes of the vineyard that he had planted, is extracted in the winepress of the cross. When men receive it with believing hearts, like capacious wineskins, it ferments within them by its own power.

And so, now that you have escaped from the power of Egypt and of Pharaoh, who is the devil, join with us, all of you, in receiving this sacrifice of the saving passover with the eagerness of dedicated hearts. Then in our inmost being we shall be wholly sanctified by the very Lord Jesus Christ whom we believe to be present in his sacraments, and whose boundless power abides for ever.

THE BREAD OF HEAVEN AND
THE CUP OF SALVATION

[*From the Jerusalem Catecheses*]

On the night he was betrayed our Lord Jesus Christ *took bread, and when he had given thanks, he broke it and gave it to his disciples and said: "Take, eat: this is my body." He took the cup, gave thanks and said: "Take, drink: this is my blood."* Since Christ himself has declared the bread to be his body, who can have any further doubt? Since he himself has said quite categorically, *This is my blood,* who would dare to question it and say that it is not his blood?

Therefore, it is with complete assurance that we receive the bread and wine as the body and blood of Christ. His body is given to us under the symbol of bread, and his blood is given to us under the symbol of wine, in order to make us by receiving them one body and blood with him. Having his body and blood in our members, we become bearers of Christ and sharers, as Saint Peter says, in the divine nature.

Once, when speaking to the Jews, Christ said: *Unless you eat my flesh and drink my blood you shall have no life in you.* This horrified them and they left him. Not understanding his words in a spiritual way, they thought the Savior wished them to practice cannibalism.

Under the old covenant there was showbread, but it came to an end with the old dispensation to which it belonged. Under the new covenant there is bread from heaven and the cup of salvation. These sanctify both soul and body, the bread being adapted to the sanctification of the body, the Word, to the sanctification of the soul.

Do not, then, regard the eucharistic elements as ordinary bread and wine: they are in fact the body and blood of the Lord, as he himself has declared. Whatever your senses may tell you, be strong in faith.

You have been taught and you are firmly convinced that what looks and tastes like bread and wine is not bread and wine but the body and blood of Christ. You know also how David referred to this long ago when he sang: *Bread gives strength to man's heart and makes his face shine with the oil of gladness*. Strengthen your heart, then, by receiving this bread as spiritual bread, and bring joy to the face of your soul.

May purity of conscience remove the veil from the face of your soul so that by contemplating the glory of the Lord, as in a mirror, you may be transformed from glory to glory in Christ Jesus our Lord. To him be glory for ever and ever. Amen.

THE PASCHAL SACRAMENT
BRINGS TOGETHER IN UNITY OF FAITH THOSE
PHYSICALLY SEPARATED FROM EACH OTHER

Saint Athanasius, Bishop
[*From an Easter Letter*]

Brethren, how fine a thing it is to move from festival to festival, from prayer to prayer, from holy day to holy day. The time is now at hand when we enter on a new beginning: the proclamation of the blessed Passover, in which the Lord was sacrificed. We feed as on the food of life, we constantly refresh our souls with his precious blood, as from a fountain. Yet we are always thirsting, burning to be satisfied. But he himself is present for those who thirst and in his goodness invites them to the feast day. Our Savior repeats his words: *If anyone thirsts, let him come to me and drink.*

He quenched the thirst not only of those who came to him then. Whenever anyone seeks him he is freely admitted to the presence of the Savior. The grace of the feast is not restricted to one occasion. Its rays of glory never set. It is always at hand to enlighten the mind of those who desire it. Its power is always there for those whose minds have been enlightened and who meditate day and night on the holy Scriptures, like the one who is called blessed in the holy psalm: *Blessed is the man who has not followed the counsel for the wicked, or stood where sinners stand, or sat in the seat of the scornful, but whose delight is in the law of the Lord, and who meditates on his law day and night.*

Moreover, my friends, the God who first established this feast for us allows us to celebrate it each year. He who gave up his Son to death for our salvation, from the same motive gives us this feast, which is commemorated every year. This feast guides us through the trials that meet us in this world. God now gives us the joy of salvation that shines out from this feast, as he brings us together to form one assembly, uniting us all in spirit in every place, allowing us to pray together and to offer common thanksgiving, as is our duty on the feast. Such is the wonder of his love: he gathers to this feast those who are far apart, and brings together in unity of faith those who may be physically separated from each other.

8

The Spirit Dwelling Within

THE SENDING OF THE HOLY SPIRIT

Saint Irenaeus, Bishop

[*From a Treatise "Against Heresies"*]

When the Lord told his disciples *to go and teach all nations* and to *baptize them in the name of the Father and of the Son and of the Holy Spirit,* he conferred on them the power of giving men new life in God.

He had promised through the prophets that in these last days he would pour out his Spirit on his servants and handmaids, and that they would prophesy. So when the Son of God became the Son of Man, the Spirit also descended upon him, becoming accustomed in this way to dwelling with the human race, to living in men and to inhabiting God's creation. The Spirit accomplished the Father's will in men who had grown old in sin, and gave them new life in Christ.

Luke says that the Spirit came down on the disciples at Pentecost, after the Lord's ascension, with power to open the gates of life to all nations and to make known to them the new covenant. So it was that men of every language joined in singing one song of praise to God, and scattered tribes, restored to unity by the Spirit, were offered to the Father as the firstfruits of all the nations.

This was why the Lord had promised to send the Advocate: he was to prepare us as an offering to God. Like dry flour, which cannot become one lump of dough, one loaf of bread, without moisture, we who are many could not become one in Christ Jesus without the water that comes down from heaven. And like parched ground, which yields no harvest unless it receives moisture, we who were once like a waterless tree could never have lived and borne fruit without this abundant rainfall from above. Through the baptism that liberates us from change and decay we have become one in body; through the Spirit we have become one in soul.

The Spirit of wisdom and understanding, the Spirit of counsel and strength, the Spirit of knowledge and the fear of God came down upon the Lord, and the Lord in turn gave this Spirit to his Church, sending the Advocate from heaven into all the world into which, according to his own words, the devil too had been cast down like lightning.

If we are not to be scorched and made unfruitful, we need the dew of God. Since we have our accuser, we need an Advocate as well. And so the Lord in his pity for man, who had fallen into the hands of brigands, having himself bound up his wounds and left for his care two coins bearing the royal image, entrusted him to the Holy Spirit. Now, through the Spirit, the image and inscription of the Father and the Son have been given to us, and it is our duty to use the coin committed to our charge and make it yield a rich profit for the Lord. ⟨≈⟩

THE FATHER'S GIFT IN CHRIST

Saint Hilary, Bishop
[*From the Treatise "On the Trinity"*]

Our Lord commanded us to baptize in the name of the Father and of the Son and of the Holy Spirit. In baptism, then, we profess faith in the creator, in the only-begotten Son and in the gift which is the Spirit. There is one Creator of all things, for in God there is one Father from whom all things have their being. And there is one only-begotten Son, our Lord Jesus Christ, through whom all things exist. And there is one Spirit, the gift who is in all. So all follow their due order, according to the proper operation of each: one power, which brings all things into being, one Son, through whom all things come to be, and one gift of perfect hope. Nothing is wanting to this flawless union: in Father, Son and Holy Spirit, there is infinity of endless being, perfect reflection of the divine image, and mutual enjoyment of the gift.

Our Lord has described the purpose of the Spirit's presence in us. Let us listen to his words: *I have yet many things to say to you, but you cannot bear them now. It is to your advantage that I go away; if I go, I will send you the*

Advocate. And also: *I will ask the Father and he will give you another Counselor to be with you for ever, the Spirit of truth. He will guide you into all the truth; for he will not speak on his own authority, but whatever he hears he will speak, and he will declare to you the things that are to come. He will glorify me, for he will take what is mine.*

From among many of our Lord's sayings, these have been chosen to guide our understanding, for they reveal to us the intention of the giver, the nature of the gift and the condition for its reception. Since our weak minds cannot comprehend the Father or the Son, we have been given the Holy Spirit as our intermediary and advocate, to shed light on that hard doctrine of our faith, the incarnation of God.

We receive the Spirit of truth so that we can know the things of God. In order to grasp this, consider how useless the faculties of the human body would become if they were denied their exercise. Our eyes cannot fulfill their task without light, either natural or artificial; our ears cannot react without sound vibrations, and in the absence of any odor our nostrils are ignorant of their function. Not that these senses would lose their own nature if they were not used; rather, they demand objects of experience in order to function. It is the same with the human soul. Unless it absorbs the gift of the Spirit through faith, the mind has the ability to know God but lacks the light necessary for that knowledge.

This unique gift which is in Christ is offered in its fullness to everyone. It is everywhere available, but it is given to each man in proportion to his readiness to receive it.

Its presence is the fuller, the greater a man's desire to be worthy of it. This gift will remain with us until the end of the world, and will be our comfort in the time of waiting. By the favors it bestows, it is the pledge of our hope for the future, the light of our minds, and the splendor that irradiates our understanding. ∾

IF I DO NOT GO AWAY, THE COMFORTER WILL NOT COME TO YOU

Saint Cyril of Alexandria, Bishop
[*From a Commentary on the Gospel of John*]

After Christ had completed his mission on earth, it still remained necessary for us to become sharers in the divine nature of the Word. We had to give up our own life and be so transformed that we would begin to live an entirely new kind of life that would be pleasing to God. This was something we could do only by sharing in the Holy Spirit.

It was most fitting that the sending of the Spirit and his descent upon us should take place after the departure of Christ our Savior. As long as Christ was with them in the flesh, it must have seemed to believers that they possessed every blessing in him; but when the time came for him to ascend to his heavenly Father, it was necessary for him to be united through his Spirit to those who worshipped him, and to dwell in our hearts through faith.

Only by his own presence within us in this way could he give us confidence to cry out, *Abba, Father*, make it easy for us to grow in holiness and, through our possession of the all-powerful Spirit, fortify us invincibly against the wiles of the devil and the assaults of men.

It can easily be shown from examples both in the Old Testament and the New that the Spirit changes those in whom he comes to dwell; he so transforms them that they begin to live a completely new kind of life. Saul was told by the prophet Samuel: *The Spirit of the Lord will take possession of you, and you shall be changed into another man.* Saint Paul writes: *As we behold the glory of the Lord with unveiled faces, that glory, which comes from the Lord who is the Spirit, transforms us all into his own likeness, from one degree of glory to another.*

Does this not show that the Spirit changes those in whom he comes to dwell and alters the whole pattern of their lives? With the Spirit within them it is quite natural for people who had been absorbed by the things of this world to become entirely other-worldly in outlook, and for cowards to become men of great courage. There can be no doubt that this is what happened to the disciples. The strength they received from the Spirit enabled them to hold firmly to the love of Christ, facing the violence of their persecutors unafraid. Very true, then, was our Savior's saying that it was to their advantage for him to return to heaven: his return was the time appointed for the descent of the Holy Spirit. ❧

THE WORK OF THE HOLY SPIRIT

Saint Basil the Great, Bishop
[*From the Treatise "On the Holy Spirit"*]

The titles given to the Holy Spirit must surely stir the soul of anyone who hears them, and make him realize that they speak of nothing less than the supreme Being. Is he not called the Spirit of God, the Spirit of truth who proceeds from the Father, the steadfast Spirit, the guiding Spirit? But his principal and most personal title is the Holy Spirit.

To the Spirit all creatures turn in their need for sanctification; all living things seek him according to their ability. His breath empowers each to achieve its own natural end.

The Spirit is the source of holiness, a spiritual light, and he offers his own light to every mind to help it in its search for truth. By nature the Spirit is beyond the reach of our mind, but we can know him by his goodness. The power of the Spirit fills the whole universe, but he gives himself only to those who are worthy, acting in each according to the measure of his faith.

Simple in himself, the Spirit is manifold in his mighty works. The whole of his being is present to each individual; the whole of his being is present everywhere. Though shared in by many, he remains unchanged; his self-giving is no loss to himself. Like the sunshine, which permeates all the atmosphere, spreading over land

and sea, and yet is enjoyed by each person as though it were for him alone, so the Spirit pours forth his grace in full measure, sufficient for all, and yet is present as though exclusively to everyone who can receive him. To all creatures that share in him he gives a delight limited only by their own nature, not by his ability to give.

The Spirit raises our hearts to heaven, guides the steps of the weak, and brings to perfection those who are making progress. He enlightens those who have been cleansed from every stain of sin and makes them spiritual by communion with himself.

As clear, transparent substances become very bright when sunlight falls on them and shine with a new radiance, so also souls in whom the Spirit dwells, and who are enlightened by the Spirit, become spiritual themselves and a source of grace for others.

From the Spirit comes foreknowledge of the future, understanding of the mysteries of faith, insight into the hidden meaning of Scripture, and other special gifts. Through the Spirit we become citizens of heaven, we are admitted to the company of the angels, we enter into eternal happiness, and abide in God. Through the Spirit we acquire a likeness to God; indeed, we attain what is beyond our most sublime aspirations — we become God.

THE LIVING WATER OF THE HOLY SPIRIT

Saint Cyril of Jerusalem, Bishop
[*From a Catechetical Instruction*]

The water that I shall give them will become in him a fountain of living water, welling up into eternal life. This is a new kind of water, a living, leaping water, welling up for those who are worthy. But why did Christ call the grace of the Spirit water? Because all things are dependent on water; plants and animals have their origin in water. Water comes down from heaven as rain, and although it is always the same in itself, it produces many different effects, one in the palm tree, another in the vine, and so on throughout the whole of creation. It does not come down, now as one thing, now as another, but while remaining essentially the same, it adapts itself to the needs of every creature that receives it.

In the same way the Holy Spirit, whose nature is always the same, simple and indivisible, apportions grace to each man as he wills. Like a dry tree which puts forth shoots when watered, the soul bears the fruit of holiness when repentance has made it worthy of receiving the Holy Spirit. Although the Spirit never changes, the effects of his action, by the will of God and in the name of Christ, are both many and marvelous.

The Spirit makes one man a teacher of divine truth, inspires another to prophesy, gives another the power of casting out devils, enables another to interpret holy Scripture. The Spirit strengthens one man's self-control, shows another how to help the poor, teaches another to fast and lead a life of asceticism, makes another oblivious to the needs of the body, trains another for martyrdom. His action is different in different people, but the Spirit himself is always the same. *In each person*, Scripture says, *the Spirit reveals his presence in a particular way for the common good.*

The Spirit comes gently and makes himself known by his fragrance. He is not felt as a burden, for he is light, very light. Rays of light and knowledge stream before him as he approaches. The Spirit comes with the tenderness of a true friend and protector to save, to heal, to teach, to counsel, to strengthen, to console. The Spirit comes to enlighten the mind first of the one who receives him, and then, through him, the minds of others as well.

As light strikes the eyes of a man who comes out of darkness into the sunshine and enables him to see clearly things he could not discern before, so light floods the soul of the man counted worthy of receiving the Holy Spirit and enables him to see things beyond the range of human vision, things hitherto undreamed of.

THE GLORY YOU GAVE TO ME, I HAVE GIVEN TO THEM

Saint Gregory of Nyssa, Bishop
[*From a Homily on the Song of Songs*]

When love has entirely cast out fear, and fear has been transformed into love, then the unity brought us by our Savior will be fully realized, for all men will be united with one another through their union with the one supreme Good. They will possess the perfection ascribed to the dove, according to our interpretation of the text: *One alone is my dove, my perfect one. She is the only child of her mother, her chosen one.*

Our Lord's words in the gospel bring out the meaning of this text more clearly. After having conferred all power on his disciples by his blessing, he obtained many other gifts for them by his prayer to the Father. Among these was included the greatest gift of all, which was that they were no longer to be divided in their judgment of what was right and good, for they were all to be united to the one supreme Good. As the Apostle says, they were to be bound together with the bonds of peace in the unity that comes from the Holy Spirit. They were to be made one body and one spirit by the one hope to which they were all called. We shall do better, however, to quote the sacred words of the gospel itself. *I pray*, the Lord says, *that they all may be one; that as you, Father, are in me and I am in you, so they also may be one in us.*

Now the bond that creates this unity is glory. That the Holy Spirit is called glory no one can deny if he thinks carefully about the Lord's words: *The glory you gave to me, I have given to them*. In fact, he gave this glory to his disciples when he said to them: *Receive the Holy Spirit*. Although he had always possessed it, even before the world existed, he himself received this glory when he put on human nature. Then, when his human nature had been glorified by the Spirit, the glory of the Spirit was passed on to all his kin, beginning with his disciples. This is why he said: *The glory you gave to me, I have given to them, so that they may be one as we are one. With me in them and you in me, I want them to be perfectly one.*

Whoever has grown from infancy to manhood and attained to spiritual maturity possesses the mastery over his passions and the purity that makes it possible for him to receive the glory of the Spirit. He is that perfect dove upon whom the eyes of the bridegroom rest when he says: *One alone is my dove, my perfect one.*

THE HOLY SPIRIT RENEWS US IN BAPTISM

Didymus of Alexandria
[*From the Treatise "On the Trinity"*]

The Holy Spirit renews us in baptism through his godhead, which he shares with the Father and the

Son. Finding us in a state of deformity, the Spirit restores our original beauty and fills us with his grace, leaving no room for anything unworthy of our love. The Spirit frees us from sin and death, and changes us from the earthly men we were, men of dust and ashes, into spiritual men, sharers in the divine glory, sons and heirs of God the Father who bear a likeness to the Son and are his co-heirs and brothers, destined to reign with him and to share his glory. In place of earth the Spirit reopens heaven to us and gladly admits us into paradise, giving us even now greater honor than the angels, and by the holy waters of baptism extinguishing the unquenchable fires of hell.

We men are conceived twice: to the human body we owe our first conception, to the divine Spirit, our second. John says: *To all who received him, who believed in his name, he gave power to become children of God. These were born not by human generation, not by the desire of the flesh, not by the will of man, but of God.* All who believed in Christ, he says, received power to become children of God, that is, of the Holy Spirit, and to gain kinship with God. To show that their parent was God the Holy Spirit, he adds these words of Christ: *I give you this solemn warning, that without being born of water and the Spirit, no one can enter the kingdom of God.*

Visibly, through the ministry of priests, the font gives symbolic birth to our visible bodies. Invisibly, through the ministry of angels, the Spirit of God, whom even the mind's eye cannot see, baptizes into himself both our souls and bodies, giving them a new birth.

Speaking quite literally, and also in harmony with the words *of water and the Spirit*, John the Baptist says of Christ: *He will baptize you with the Holy Spirit and with fire.* Since we are only vessels of clay, we must first be cleansed in water and then hardened by spiritual fire — for *God is a consuming fire.* We need the Holy Spirit to perfect and renew us, for spiritual fire can cleanse us, and spiritual water can recast us as in a furnace and make us into new men. ❧

THE SPIRIT GIVES LIFE

Saint Basil the Great, Bishop
[*From the Book "On the Holy Spirit"*]

Our Lord made a covenant with us through baptism in order to give us eternal life. There is in baptism an image both of death and of life, the water being the symbol of death, the Spirit giving the pledge of life. The association of water and the Spirit is explained by the twofold purpose for which baptism was instituted, namely, to destroy the sin in us so that it could never again give birth to death, and to enable us to live by the Spirit and so win the reward of holiness. The water into which the body enters as into a tomb symbolizes death; the Spirit instills into us his life-giving power, awakening our souls from the death of sin to the life that they had in the beginning. This then is what it means to be born again of water and the Spirit: we die in the water, and we come to life again through the Spirit.

To signify this death and to enlighten the baptized by transmitting to them knowledge of God, the great sacrament of baptism is administered by means of a triple immersion and the invocation of each of the three divine Persons. Whatever grace there is in the water comes not from its own nature but from the presence of the Spirit, *since baptism is not a cleansing of the body, but a pledge made to God from a clear conscience.*

As a preparation for our life after the resurrection, our Lord tells us in the gospel how we should live here and now. He teaches us to be peaceable, long-suffering, undefiled by desire for pleasure, and detached from worldly wealth. In this way we can achieve, by our own free choice, the kind of life that will be natural in the world to come.

Through the Holy Spirit we are restored to paradise, we ascend to the kingdom of heaven, and we are reinstated as adopted sons. Thanks to the Spirit we obtain the right to call God our Father, we become sharers in the grace of Christ, we are called children of light, and we share in everlasting glory. In a word, every blessing is showered upon us, both in this world and in the world to come. As we contemplate them even now, like a reflection in a mirror, it is as though we already possessed the good things our faith tells us that we shall one day enjoy. If this is the pledge, what will the perfection be? If these are the first-fruits, what will the full harvest be?

THE ANOINTING WITH THE HOLY SPIRIT

From the Jerusalem Catecheses

When we were baptized into Christ and clothed ourselves in him, we were transformed into the likeness of the Son of God. Having destined us to be his adopted sons, God gave us a likeness to Christ in his glory, and living as we do in communion with Christ, God's anointed, we ourselves are rightly called "the anointed ones." When he said: *Do not touch my anointed ones*, God was speaking of us.

We became "the anointed ones" when we received the sign of the Holy Spirit. Indeed, everything took place in us by means of images, because we ourselves are images of Christ. Christ bathed in the river Jordan, imparting to its waters the fragrance of his divinity, and when he came up from them the Holy Spirit descended upon him, like resting upon like. So we also, after coming up from the sacred waters of baptism, were anointed with chrism, which signifies the Holy Spirit, by whom Christ was anointed and of whom blessed Isaiah prophesied in the name of the Lord: *The Spirit of the Lord is upon me, because he has anointed me. He has sent me to preach good news to the poor.*

Christ's anointing was not by human hands, nor was it with ordinary oil. On the contrary, having destined him to be the Savior of the whole world, the Father himself anointed him with the Holy Spirit. The words of

Peter bear witness to this: *Jesus of Nazareth, whom God anointed with the Holy Spirit.* And David the prophet proclaimed: *Your throne, O God, shall endure for ever; your royal scepter is a scepter of justice. You have loved righteousness and hated iniquity; therefore God, your God, has anointed you with the oil of gladness above all your fellows.*

The oil of gladness with which Christ was anointed was a spiritual oil; it was in fact the Holy Spirit himself, who is called *the oil of gladness* because he is the source of spiritual joy. But we too have been anointed with oil, and by this anointing we have entered into fellowship with Christ and have received a share in his life. Beware of thinking that this holy oil is simply ordinary oil and nothing else. After the invocation of the Spirit it is no longer ordinary oil but the gift of Christ, and by the presence of his divinity it becomes the instrument through which we receive the Holy Spirit. While symbolically, on our foreheads and senses, our bodies are anointed with this oil that we see, our souls are sanctified by the holy and life-giving Spirit. ❧

A SAMARITAN WOMAN CAME TO DRAW WATER

Saint Augustine, Bishop
[*From a Treatise on John*]

A woman came. She is a symbol of the Church not yet made righteous but about to be made righteous.

Righteousness follows from the conversation. She came in ignorance, she found Christ, and he enters into conversation with her. Let us see what it is about, let us see why *a Samaritan woman came to draw water.* The Samaritans did not form part of the Jewish people: they were foreigners. The fact that she came from a foreign people is part of the symbolic meaning, for she is a symbol of the Church. The Church was to come from the Gentiles, of a different race from the Jews.

We must then recognize ourselves in her words and in her person, and with her give our own thanks to God. She was a symbol, not the reality; she foreshadowed the reality, and the reality came to be. She found faith in Christ, who was using her as a symbol to teach us what was to come. *She came* then *to draw water.* She had simply come to draw water, in the normal way of man or woman.

Jesus says to her: Give me water to drink. For his disciples had gone to the city to buy food. The Samaritan woman therefore says to him: How is it that you, though a Jew, ask me for water to drink, though I am a Samaritan woman? For Jews have nothing to do with Samaritans.

The Samaritans were foreigners; Jews never used their utensils. The woman was carrying a pail for drawing water. She was astonished that a Jew should ask her for a drink of water, a thing that Jews would not do. But the one who was asking for a drink of water was thirsting for her faith.

Listen now and learn who it is that asks for a drink. *Jesus answered her and said: If you knew the gift of God, and who it is that is saying to you, "Give me a drink," perhaps you might have asked him and he would have given you living water.*

He asks for a drink, and he promises a drink. He is in need, as one hoping to receive, yet he is rich, as one about to satisfy the thirst of others. He says: *If you knew the gift of God.* The gift of God is the Holy Spirit. But he is still using veiled language as he speaks to the woman and gradually enters into her heart. Or is he already teaching her? What could be more gentle and kind than the encouragement he gives. *If you knew the gift of God, and who it is that is saying to you, "Give me a drink," perhaps you might ask and he would give you living water.*

What is this water that he will give if not the water spoken of in Scripture: *With you is the fountain of life?* How can those feel thirst who *will drink deeply from the abundance in your house?*

He was promising the Holy Spirit in satisfying abundance. She did not yet understand. In her failure to grasp his meaning, what was her reply? *The woman says to him: Master, give me this drink, so that I may feel no thirst or come here to draw water.* Her need forced her to this labor, her weakness shrank from it. If only she could hear those words: *Come to me, all who labor and are burdened, and I will refresh you.* Jesus was saying this to her, so that her labors might be at an end; but she was not yet able to understand.

9

Biographical Index of Authors

St. Anastasius of Antioch (died 599) was a patriarch
of Antioch. He was banished from his see by Emperor
Justin II for opposing several imperial decrees about the
body of Christ, but was restored twenty-three years
later, in 573, by Pope Gregory the Great.

St. Andrew of Crete (c. 660-c. 740) was born in
Damascus and became archbishop of Gortyna, Crete.
He was famous for his preaching and for writing hymns.

St. Asterius of Amasea (died around 410) was born in
Pontus in Asia Minor, became a rhetorician, and then
was ordained and made bishop of Amasea. He was
noted for his preaching, and twenty-one of his sermons
are still in existence.

St. Athanasius (c. 297-373) is known as the champion
of orthodoxy for his tireless defense of the faith against
the Arian heresy. He was born in Alexandria and was
elected bishop of that city about 327. As bishop, he
was exiled five times by emperors who sided with the
Arians. He wrote the famous *On the Incarnation* and
numerous other theological works.

St. Augustine (354-430) was born at Thagaste in Northern Africa to a Christian mother and pagan father. As a young man, he joined a heretical sect but converted to Christianity in 387. He was ordained in 391 and made bishop of Hippo in 395. Augustine wrote prolifically on doctrine and scripture, and is considered the most influential theologian in the history of Christianity. He is a Doctor of the Church.

St. Basil the Great (329-379) was born in Caesarea, Cappadocia in Asia Minor. He became a hermit in 358 and, after attracting disciples, organized the first monastery in Asia Minor. As archbishop, he helped the poor and sick, and encouraged the clergy to live holy lives. His treatises and other works, including *On the Holy Spirit*, have greatly influenced Christian doctrine. He is a Doctor of the Church.

St. Clement I (died around 99) was, according to tradition, baptized by St. Peter. He became pope in 91, and was exiled by the Emperor Trajan but continued preaching to his fellow prisoners in Crimea. Scholars agree that he authored a letter to the Corinthians rebuking them for a split in their church. He died in exile.

St. Cyril of Alexandria (c. 376-444) was born in Alexandria, Egypt, and was made patriarch of that city in 412. He fought against the Nestorian heresy, and wrote treatises that clarified the doctrines of the Trinity and the Incarnation. He was declared a Doctor of the Church in 1882.

St. Cyril of Jerusalem (c. 315-386) was born of Christian parents and raised in Jerusalem. He became bishop of Jerusalem in 349 and was exiled three times by Arian supporters but returned to his see each time. He was a scripture scholar and author of the *Catecheses*, which outlined the instructions for people preparing for baptism. He was declared a Doctor of the Church in 1882.

Didymus of Alexandria (c. 313-died between 395 and 399) became blind as a child, but his progress in theology was so great that he amazed his contemporaries. A disciple of Origen, he wrote three books on the Trinity in addition to extensive treatises on almost every book in the Bible.

St. Ephrem of Syria (c. 306-c. 373) was born at Nisibis in Mesopotamia and baptized at the age of eighteen. When Nisibis was ceded to Persia in 363, he began living in a cave near Edessa in Roman territory, where he wrote prolifically on doctrinal issues, including the Last Judgment. He introduced hymns into public worship. He was declared a Doctor of the Church in 1920.

St. Fulgentius of Ruspe (468-533) was born of a noble family in Carthage and became a monk when he was twenty-two years old. In 499, he was arrested by an Arian priest and tortured, then released. Appointed bishop of Ruspe in Tunisia in 508, he was banished twice at the instigation of Arian bishops. His treatises defending the orthodox position so influenced the king that he was permitted for a short while to return to his see.

St. Gaudentius of Brescia (died around 410) was born in Brescia, Italy, and became a monk at Caesarea in Cappadocia. He was consecrated bishop of Brescia in 387, and was one of three bishops sent by the pope to defend St. John Chrysostom before the emperor in 405. The bishops were imprisoned but then freed. He died in Italy.

St. Gregory Nazianzen (c. 329-389) was born in Nazianzus in Cappadocia, and ordained in 362 by his father, who was bishop. When a group of bishops invited him to Constantinople to help restore orthodoxy, his eloquent preaching led many Arians to convert. He was named archbishop of Constantinople in 380, but resigned shortly afterward when the validity of his election was questioned. He is known for his great defenses of orthodoxy and the decrees of the Nicene Council.

St. Gregory the Great (c. 540-604) was born and educated in Rome, and became a monk. However, he was called out of seclusion in 578 to serve the pope. Himself elected pope in 590, he governed wisely and was generous to the poor. He sent St. Augustine of Canterbury to convert the English, and restored Rome, which had suffered from invasions and earthquakes. He wrote hundreds of sermons and letters along with many treatises. He was canonized immediately after his death, and is a Doctor of the Church.

St. Gregory of Nyssa (c. 330-c. 395) was the brother of St. Basil and was born at Caesarea, Cappadocia. Educated in rhetoric, he became a teacher but was disenchanted by his students and was ordained a priest. He was named bishop of Nyssa, Lower Armenia, in 372, but was imprisoned and exiled by Arians. He wrote many treatises and was considered a great defender of orthodoxy.

St. Hilary of Poitiers (died around 368) was born in Poitiers, Gaul, into a noble family. He was already an older man and married when he converted to Christianity. He was elected bishop of Poitiers around 350, and became immersed in the Arian controversy. He was exiled for several years for his defense of orthodoxy. He wrote numerous treatises, including *On the Trinity*, and was declared a Doctor of the Church in 1851.

St. Irenaeus (c. 125-c. 203) was born in Asia Minor and sent by St. Polycarp as a missionary to Gaul, where he evangelized the area around Lyons. He became bishop of Lyons in 178 after the previous bishop was martyred in a Christian persecution. He strongly opposed the Gnostic heresy, and his five-book treatise against Gnosticism earned him a reputation as a great theologian.

Blessed Isaac of Stella (c. 1100-c. 1169) was born in England and worked for the archbishop of Canterbury before entering Citeaux, a Cistercian monastery in France, in 1145. He was chosen abbot of Stella, another Cistercian abbey, two years later. Among his sermons are those given to a group of monks during Lent on a solitary island. In 1162, he wrote an epistle on the soul.

St. John Chrysostom (c. 347-407) was born in Antioch, Syria. After his ordination in 386, he became famous for his preaching (Chrysostom means "golden-mouthed"), along with his homilies on the books of the New Testament. He was made Patriarch of Constantinople in 398, and his denunciations of the extravagant lifestyles of the ruling class led to his exile, where he eventually died. He was declared a Doctor of the universal Church at the Council of Chalcedon in 451.

St. Justin Martyr (c. 100-c. 165) was the first
Christian apologist who wrote extensively about
Christianity. Born in Flavia Neapolis of pagan parents,
he became a Christian at the age of thirty. He opened a
school of philosophy in Rome and debated pagan
philosophers. He was reported as a Christian to Roman
authorities and, after refusing to sacrifice to the gods,
was beheaded.

St. Leo the Great (died 461) was born in Rome and
elected to the papacy in 440, after serving as deacon
under the previous two popes. He delivered a famous
series of ninety-six sermons, and clarified the doctrine
of the incarnation at the Council of Chalcedon. After
barbarians attacked Rome, he helped to rebuild the
city. He was named a Doctor of the Church in 1754.

St. Maximus the Confessor (c. 580-662) was born into
a noble family in Constantinople and became a monk.
As a leader against a heresy called Monothelitism, he
was seized at a council in Rome, charged with conspir-
acy against the empire, and exiled. After suffering tor-
ture and mutilation, he died. In addition to biblical
commentaries and treatises, he wrote extensively about
mysticism.

St. Maximus of Turin (c. 380-c. 467) was a preacher and biblical scholar who wrote hundreds of sermons, homilies and other works, many of which are still in existence. He was born in Vercelli, Italy, and became bishop of Turin.

St. Melito of Sardis (died around 180) was bishop of Sardis in Lydia, and became famous for his many theological treatises, including a defense of Christianity to Emperor Marcus Aurelius.

Origen (185-254) was born in Alexandria. At a young age, he became a teacher and directed a catechetical school. He traveled widely and was ordained by the bishop of Jerusalem, but was subsequently banished by his own bishop for being ordained outside his see. He settled in Caesarea, and continued to teach and write his many biblical commentaries, letters and homilies— several thousand in all. He was tortured in a Christian persecution and died several years later.

St. Peter Chrysologus (406-c. 450) was born in Imola, Italy, and was named bishop of Ravenna in 433. His preaching made such an impact on the empress that she enthusiastically supported his building projects. Noted for his homilies (Chrysologus means "golden-worded"), he was named a Doctor of the Church in 1729.

Tertullian (c. 155-c. 220) was born in Carthage, and was an advocate in the Roman courts of law when he converted to Christianity in 193. He was a brilliant writer whose works have preserved a window into the beliefs and worship of the early church. In 207, he broke with the church and joined the Montanists in Africa, and later formed his own party.

St. Theodore the Studite (759-826) was born in Constantinople. He became a monk and eventually was made abbot of the famous Studios Monastery in Constantinople, which under his direction grew to become a center of Eastern monastic life. He was exiled and imprisoned several times for denouncing various actions of the emperor.

St. Theophilus of Antioch (dates unknown) was a bishop of Antioch in the late second century. His only writing still in existence consists of three books titled *To Autolycus*, which address objections to Christianity and discuss the doctrine of creation.

Other titles from The Word Among Us Press Wisdom Series

A Radical Love:
   Wisdom from Dorothy Day

Welcoming the New Millennium:
   Wisdom from Pope John Paul II

My Heart Speaks:
   Wisdom from Pope John XXIII

Live Jesus! Wisdom from Saints Francis
   de Sales and Jane de Chantal

Love Songs:
   Wisdom from St. Bernard of Clairvaux

Walking with the Father:
   Wisdom from Brother Lawrence

Even unto Death:
   Wisdom from Modern Martyrs

Hold Fast to God:
   Wisdom from The Early Church

These popular books include short biographies of the authors and selections from their writings grouped around themes such as prayer, forgiveness, and mercy.

**To order call 1-800-775-9673
or order online at www.wau.org**